100 Dishes For Two

100
Dishes
For Two

Edited by
Rhona Newman

octopus

Contents

NOTES

Standard spoon measurements are used in all recipes
1 tablespoon = one 15 ml spoon
1 teaspoon = one 5 ml spoon
All spoon measures are level.

Fresh herbs are used unless otherwise stated. If unobtainable, substitute a bouquet garni of the equivalent dried herbs, or use dried herbs instead but halve the quantities stated.

Ovens and grills (broilers) should be preheated to the specified temperature or heat setting.

For all recipes, quantities are given in metric, imperial and American measures. Follow one set of measures only, because they are not interchangeable.

First published 1982 by
Octopus Books Limited
59 Grosvenor Street, London W1

© 1982 Octopus Books Limited

ISBN 0 7064 1769 0

Produced by Mandarin Publishers Ltd
22a Westlands Rd
Quarry Bay, Hong Kong

Printed in Hong Kong

Frontispiece: Minted Melon and Strawberry Cocktail (page 40)

Introduction

When you have to cook for just two people, there is often a tendency to serve quick convenience-type meals or even rely on the services of the local take-away. But with a little imagination and planning, cooking for two can be just as interesting and rewarding as cooking for a crowd.

The recipes in this book aim to provide attractive, tasty and nutritious dishes for two with quantities which avoid any waste. Sometimes it is a good idea to cook extra rice, pasta, potatoes or other vegetables as they can be used in salads or nutritious snack meals the next day. It can also be useful to cook larger pieces of meat such as a roast or a whole chicken as then the leftover meat can be used for another meal.

Fish should not be overlooked when cooking for two as it is a versatile and nutritious food. It requires less cooking than meat and can be bought in convenient-size pieces. Although there are now less wet fish shops and stalls around, most supermarkets have packets of frozen fish in their deep freeze cabinets. These are conveniently packaged and portioned in various sizes and the extra cost is often worthwhile as there is no waste on frozen fish.

Whether cooking for one, two or more, it is very important to have a varied and balanced diet, preferably based on three meals a day without too many in between snacks! Breakfast is important and you will feel much better if you eat something before rushing out of the house. Try fresh orange juice and a bowl of cereal; yogurt sprinkled with bran; wholemeal bread and a slice of cheese; toast spread with peanut butter or cheese spread; or a glass of plain or flavoured milk.

It is important to include protein or body-building foods at each meal. These include meat, poultry, fish, eggs, cheese, nuts and pulses. Include a portion of vegetables and fruit to provide vitamins and minerals, plus bread, potatoes or cereals to satisfy the appetite. This latter group of foods are known as carbohydrates and they provide us with energy. Most carbohydrates, with the exception of sugar, contain some useful nutrients, but generally if eaten in excess, this group of foods will add the extra kilograms or pounds! Furthermore, these foods are often eaten with fats, which again, if eaten in excess can add extra weight and may lead to other health problems.

Convenience foods can be useful on some occasions as they save time and avoid waste when only small quantities are required. The best results are achieved if you combine convenience foods with fresh foods.

Shopping should be carefully planned each week to save time and effort. Work out menus for each day and make a shopping list. Buy a few extras for the store cupboard and freezer as frozen foods, cans and packets all make useful standbys. Try to build up a supply of canned tomatoes, sweetcorn, fish, soups, meat and fruits; packets of rice, pasta, dried fruits, cake mixes, sauce mixes, stuffings and dried potato; also herbs, spices, sauces and flavourings. If you own a freezer, keep a supply of vegetables, fruit, small cuts of meat and fish and ice cream. Vegetables and fruit are cheaper bought from markets or greengrocer shops than in a supermarket. Also, making use of the vegetables and fruit in season often saves money.

Entertaining for two can be a pleasant and relaxing way to enjoy a meal. Try the recipes and menu ideas at the end of the book, or take recipes from other sections to make up your own menus. Snacks such as Mackerel Spread or Quick Liver Pâté can be used as a starter or try Stuffed Peppers or Avocado and Apple Salad. Choose a main course from the Main Meals section and a dessert such as Caribbean Coffee Creams, Jamaican Meringue or Mock Chocolate Mousse.

Whatever your likes, dislikes and way of life, the recipes in this book should give you plenty of scope for interesting and healthy eating.

Quick Snack Meals

There are often times when a meal is required very quickly. For a nutritious snack, try the fried sandwiches or the Quick French Bread Pizza. These and the other recipes make good use of leftovers, convenience foods and standbys such as bread, eggs and cheese. Other recipes in this chapter are sufficient for a meal with the suggested accompaniments. Most of them are very quick and simple to make and take no longer than 30 to 40 minutes to cook – many of them much less!

Pitta Parcels

METRIC/IMPERIAL	AMERICAN
2 pitta breads	2 pitta breads
1 × 113 g/4 oz carton coleslaw	1 cup coleslaw
225 g/8 oz cod fillet, skinned	½ lb cod fillet, skinned
1 egg, beaten	1 egg, beaten
40 g/1½ oz dry breadcrumbs	½ cup dry bread crumbs
oil for deep frying	oil for deep frying

Cut each piece of pitta bread in half lengthwise using a sharp knife. Keep the halves whole and split open.

Place 1 tablespoon coleslaw in the bottom of each half. Cut the fish into strips and dip into the egg then the breadcrumbs.

Heat the oil in a deep fat frying pan to 190°C/375°F (when a piece of bread browns in just under 1 minute) and fry the fish for 2 to 3 minutes. Drain on kitchen paper towels.

Divide the fish between the pitta breads and serve immediately with some mayonnaise or seafood sauce.
Cooking time: 5 minutes

Mackerel Spread

METRIC/IMPERIAL	AMERICAN
1 × 198 g/7 oz can mackerel in tomato sauce	1 × 7 oz can mackerel in tomato sauce
50 g/2 oz red Leicester cheese, grated	½ cup grated brick cheese
salt and pepper	salt and pepper
2 baps	2 baps
butter	butter

Place the mackerel with its sauce in a bowl and flake with a fork. Add the cheese and salt and pepper to taste and mix well.

Cut the baps in half and spread with butter. Pile the mackerel mixture on top and place under a preheated moderate grill (broiler) for 10 minutes or until golden brown. Serve with a crisp green salad.
Cooking time: 10 minutes
Variation:
Canned sardines or sild can be used in place of the mackerel. Vary the type of cheese for a different flavour too.

Pitta Parcels
(Photograph: Sea Fish Kitchen)

Sardine Squares

METRIC/IMPERIAL	AMERICAN
4 slices wholewheat bread	4 slices wholewheat bread
50 g/2 oz butter	¼ cup butter
1 × 119 g/4½ oz can sardines in oil	1 × 4½ oz can sardines in oil
1 tablespoon salad cream	1 tablespoon salad cream
salt and pepper	salt and pepper
2 eggs	2 eggs
2 tablespoons milk	2 tablespoons milk

Spread the bread with some of the butter. Drain the oil from the sardines into a frying pan. Mash the fish to a paste with the salad cream. Add salt and pepper to taste.

Use the fish mixture to make two sandwiches, then cut each one into quarters. Beat the eggs with the milk, salt and pepper. Dip the sandwiches into this mixture so that they are coated on both sides, then drain.

Heat the remaining butter with the sardine oil in the frying pan, add the sandwiches and fry for 5 to 8 minutes, turning once to ensure even browning. Drain and serve immediately with celery sticks and cucumber.
Cooking time: 5 to 8 minutes

Quick Liver Pâté

METRIC/IMPERIAL	AMERICAN
75 g/3 oz liver sausage	⅓ cup liver sausage
25 g/1 oz soft margarine	2 tablespoons soft margarine
25 g/1 oz cream cheese	2 tablespoons cream cheese
1 tablespoon cream	1 tablespoon cream
1 teaspoon lemon juice	1 teaspoon lemon juice
salt and freshly ground black pepper	salt and freshly ground black pepper
2 stuffed olives to garnish	2 stuffed olives for garnish

Place the liver sausage in a bowl and blend in the margarine and cream cheese. Stir in the cream, lemon juice, salt and pepper to taste and mix well. Spoon into two individual dishes and smooth the tops.

Slice the olives and use to garnish the pâté. Serve with toast or bread rolls and tomatoes.

Dutch Open Sandwiches

METRIC/IMPERIAL	AMERICAN
2 slices rye bread	2 slices rye bread
butter	butter
2 slices ham	2 slices ham
75 g/3 oz Gouda cheese, grated	¾ cup grated Gouda cheese
Garnish:	**Garnish:**
cucumber slices	cucumber slices
red pepper rings	red pepper rings
parsley sprigs	parsley sprigs

Spread the bread with butter. Arrange the ham slices on top, then the grated cheese. Garnish each elaborately with the cucumber, red pepper and parsley. These sandwiches are easier to eat with a knife and fork.
Variations:
Use the ham and cheese as a base, then add a selection of the following toppings: tomato slices; mustard and cress; shredded lettuce; halved green olives; gherkin fans; spring onions (scallions); watercress; red cabbage; green pepper rings; walnuts; pineapple rings; cocktail cherries; radish slices.

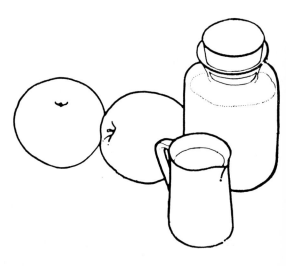

Sage and Onion Twin Bake

METRIC/IMPERIAL	AMERICAN
½ × 113 g/4 oz packet sage and onion stuffing mix	½ × ¼ lb package sage and onion stuffing mix
150 ml/¼ pint boiling water	⅔ cup boiling water
15 g/½ oz butter	1 tablespoon butter
1 tablespoon milk	1 tablespoon milk
salt and pepper	salt and pepper
150 g/5 oz mashed potato	⅔ cup mashed potato
2 eggs	2 eggs
1 tomato, sliced	1 tomato, sliced

Combine the stuffing mix with the boiling water and add the butter and milk. Add salt and pepper to taste.

Combine the stuffing mixture with the potato and spread into a greased shallow ovenproof dish. Make two hollows in the mixture and break an egg into each.

Arrange the tomato slices at each end and cook in a preheated moderately hot oven (190°C/375°F, Gas Mark 5) for 15 to 20 minutes or until the eggs are cooked. Serve immediately.

Cooking time: 15 to 20 minutes

Quick French Bread Pizza

METRIC/IMPERIAL	AMERICAN
½ small French loaf	½ small French loaf
1 tablespoon tomato purée	1 tablespoon tomato paste
1 × 227 g/8 oz can tomatoes, drained	1 × 8 oz can tomatoes, drained
50 g/2 oz cooked ham, diced	¼ cup diced cooked ham
50 g/2 oz button mushrooms, sliced	½ cup sliced button mushrooms
1 teaspoon oil	1 teaspoon oil
50 g/2 oz Mozzarella cheese, sliced	2 oz Mozzarella cheese, sliced
salt and pepper	salt and pepper

Split the French bread lengthwise into two pieces. Spread each piece with tomato purée (paste). Chop the tomatoes and arrange on the bread with the ham and mushrooms. Brush these with oil then top with the cheese.

Sprinkle with salt and pepper and place under a preheated moderate grill (broiler) for 5 minutes until the cheese is bubbling and golden brown. Serve immediately with salad.

Cooking time: 5 to 8 minutes

Variation:

If French bread is not available, make the pizzas with baps or toast.

Edam Sausage Pasties

METRIC/IMPERIAL	AMERICAN
½ × 215 g/7½ oz packet frozen puff pastry, thawed	½ × 7½ oz package frozen puff pastry, thawed
100 g/4 oz pork sausagemeat	½ cup pork sausage meat
1 celery stick, finely chopped	1 stalk celery, minced
50 g/2 oz Edam cheese, grated	½ cup grated Edam cheese
1 small apple	1 small apple
salt and pepper	salt and pepper
1 egg, beaten	1 egg, beaten

Divide the pastry in half and roll out each piece to a 15 cm/6 inch square. Trim the edges and reserve the trimmings to make pastry leaves.

Place the sausagemeat in a bowl and add the celery and cheese. Peel, core and grate the apple and add to the sausagemeat with the salt and pepper and half the beaten egg. Mix well.

Divide the filling between the squares. Brush the edges with a little of the remaining egg and fold over to make two parcels. Decorate with pastry leaves. Brush with beaten egg and place on a baking sheet.

Cook in a preheated hot oven (220°C/425°F, Gas Mark 7) for 25 to 30 minutes or until golden brown.
Cooking time: 25 to 30 minutes

Surprise Rolls

METRIC/IMPERIAL	AMERICAN
2 crusty bread rolls	2 crusty bread rolls
20 g/¾ oz butter	1½ tablespoons butter
100 g/4 oz smoked mackerel fillet	¼ lb smoked mackerel fillet
2 tablespoons baked beans	2 tablespoons baked beans
salt and pepper	salt and pepper

Cut the top off each roll and carefully remove the crumbs inside to form a hollow roll. Roughly chop the crumbs. Melt the butter in a frying pan and fry the crumbs until crisp.

Skin the mackerel and flake the fish. Add to the pan with the beans, salt and pepper. Mix well and cook for 2 to 3 minutes.

Spoon the mixture into the rolls, replace the tops and serve immediately.
Cooking time: 8 to 10 minutes

Edam and Salami Pizza

METRIC/IMPERIAL	AMERICAN
Base:	**Base:**
50 g/2 oz slightly salted butter	¼ cup slightly salted butter
225 g/8 oz self-raising flour	2 cups self-rising flour
pinch of salt	pinch of salt
50 g/2 oz Edam cheese, grated	½ cup grated Edam cheese
150 ml/¼ pint milk	⅔ cup milk
Topping:	**Topping:**
1 onion, finely grated	1 onion, minced
1 × 425 g/15 oz can tomatoes, drained	1 × 16 oz can tomatoes
salt and freshly ground pepper	salt and freshly ground pepper
½ teaspoon dried mixed herbs	½ teaspoon dried mixed herbs
50 g/2 oz mushrooms, sliced	½ cup sliced mushrooms
100 g/4 oz salami, chopped	½ cup chopped salami
100 g/4 oz Edam cheese, sliced and cut into strips	4 oz Edam cheese, sliced and cut into strips
14 black olives	14 ripe olives

Rub (cut) the butter into the flour and salt until the mixture resembles fine breadcrumbs. Mix in the grated cheese, add the milk and mix to a soft dough. Divide the dough in half and roll out each half into an 18 cm/7 inch round. Place the rounds on a large greased baking sheet.

Mix together the onion, tomatoes, seasoning and herbs, breaking up the tomatoes with a fork. Spread half the mixture on to each round. Place the mushrooms and salami on top of the tomatoes and cook in a preheated hot oven (220°C/425°F, Gas Mark 7) for 15 minutes, or until the base is risen and golden brown.

Remove the pizzas from the oven and place the cheese strips in a lattice pattern on top. Return to the oven and cook for a further 5 to 10 minutes until the cheese has melted. Serve hot or cold, garnished with black olives and accompanied by a green salad.
Cooking time: 25 minutes

Edam and Salami Pizza
(Photograph: The Dutch Dairy Bureau)

Fried Cheese Sandwiches

METRIC/IMPERIAL	AMERICAN
4 thin slices bread	4 thin slices bread
butter	butter
50 g/2 oz Gouda cheese, sliced	2 oz Gouda cheese, sliced
4 tablespoons milk	4 tablespoons milk
2 tablespoons plain flour	2 tablespoons all-purpose flour
salt and pepper	salt and pepper
1 egg	1 egg
2 teaspoons oil	2 teaspoons oil
oil for deep frying	oil for deep frying

Spread the slices of bread with butter and use the cheese to make two sandwiches. Trim off all the crusts.

Dip each sandwich in the milk, then in the flour seasoned with salt and pepper. Beat together the egg and oil then dip the sandwiches into this mixture. Ensure that each sandwich is well coated and all the edges are secure.

Fill a deep fat fryer half full with oil and heat to 180°C/350°F (or when a piece of bread browns in just over 1 minute). Cook the sandwiches one at a time, turning once to ensure even browning. Serve immediately with tomato sauce or pickle.

Cooking time: 5 to 8 minutes

Salmon Pizzas

METRIC/IMPERIAL	AMERICAN
Base:	**Base:**
100 g/4 oz self-raising flour	1 cup self-rising flour
pinch of salt	pinch of salt
25 g/1 oz margarine	2 tablespoons margarine
4 tablespoons milk	4 tablespoons milk
Topping:	**Topping:**
1 × 397 g/14 oz can tomatoes, drained and chopped	1 × 16 oz can tomatoes, drained and chopped
50 g/2 oz button mushrooms, sliced	½ cup sliced button mushrooms
½ green pepper, cored, seeded and sliced	½ green pepper, seeded and sliced
2 tablespoons chopped spring onions	2 tablespoons chopped scallions
1 × 213 g/7½ oz can pink salmon, drained	1 × 7½ oz can pink salmon, drained
50 g/2 oz Cheddar cheese, grated	½ cup grated Cheddar cheese
salt and pepper	salt and pepper

Sift the flour and salt into a bowl and rub (cut) in the margarine until the mixture resembles fine breadcrumbs. Stir in the milk and mix to a firm dough. Turn onto a floured surface and knead until smooth.

Divide the dough in half and roll out each piece to a 15 cm/6 inch round. Place on a large greased baking sheet.

Arrange the tomatoes, mushrooms and green pepper on top. Sprinkle over the spring onions (scallions). Remove any skin and bones from the salmon and arrange chunks on the pizzas. Sprinkle over the grated cheese and salt and pepper to taste.

Cook in a preheated moderately hot oven (200°C/400°F, Gas Mark 6) for 15 to 20 minutes until the dough is cooked and the cheese bubbling and golden. Serve warm with salad.

Cooking time: 15 to 20 minutes

Baker's Cheese Soufflé

METRIC/IMPERIAL	AMERICAN
6 thin slices French bread	6 thin slices French bread
50 g/2 oz butter, softened	¼ cup softened butter
25 g/1 oz plain flour	¼ cup all-purpose flour
150 ml/¼ pint milk	⅔ cup milk
½ teaspoon made mustard	½ teaspoon prepared mustard
3 eggs, separated	3 eggs, separated
75 g/3 oz mature Cheddar cheese, grated	¾ cup grated mature Cheddar cheese
salt and pepper	salt and pepper

Spread both sides of the bread with half the butter and use to line a greased 900 ml/1½ pint (3¾ cup) soufflé dish.

Melt the remaining 25 g/1 oz (2 tablespoons) butter in a pan, stir in the flour and cook for 1 minute. Remove from the heat and gradually blend in the milk. Heat, stirring, until the sauce thickens. Cool slightly then beat in the mustard and egg yolks. Stir in the cheese and add salt and pepper to taste.

Whisk the egg whites until just stiff and carefully fold into the cheese mixture. Pour into the soufflé dish. Cook in a preheated moderately hot oven (200°C/400°F, Gas Mark 6) for 30 minutes or until well risen and golden brown. Serve immediately with salad.
Cooking time: 35 to 40 minutes

Mediterranean Omelette

METRIC/IMPERIAL	AMERICAN
15 g/½ oz margarine	1 tablespoon margarine
1 onion, chopped	1 onion, chopped
50 g/2 oz mushrooms, sliced	½ cup sliced mushrooms
1 red pepper, cored, seeded and chopped	1 red pepper, seeded and chopped
1 garlic clove, crushed	1 garlic clove, minced
2 tomatoes, skinned and chopped	2 tomatoes, peeled and chopped
3 eggs	3 eggs
2 teaspoons water	2 teaspoons water
1 teaspoon mixed herbs	1 teaspoon mixed herbs
salt and pepper	salt and pepper
2 teaspoons oil	2 teaspoons oil
25 g/1 oz grated Parmesan cheese	¼ cup grated Parmesan cheese
watercress to garnish	watercress for garnish

Melt the margarine in a pan and sauté the onion, mushrooms, red pepper, garlic and tomatoes for 5 to 10 minutes or until soft.

Beat the eggs with the water, herbs and salt and pepper to taste. Heat the oil in an omelette pan and pour in the egg mixture. Cook over a medium heat for 1 minute or until the mixture is set on the bottom.

Spoon the vegetables over the omelette and continue to cook for 1 to 2 minutes. Sprinkle with Parmesan cheese, cut into two and serve immediately, garnished with watercress.
Cooking time: 14 minutes

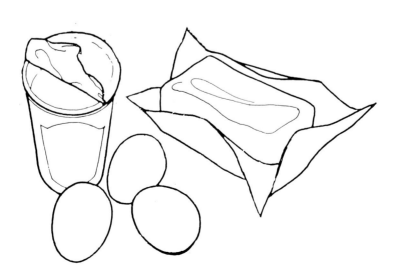

Eggs Sweet and Sour

METRIC/IMPERIAL	AMERICAN
25 g/1 oz butter	2 tablespoons butter
1 green pepper, cored, seeded and chopped	1 green pepper, seeded and chopped
1 onion, sliced	1 onion, sliced
2 celery sticks, chopped	2 stalks celery, chopped
1 × 210 g/7½ oz can pineapple pieces	1 × 7½ oz can pineapple pieces
1 tablespoon tomato purée	1 tablespoon tomato paste
1 teaspoon cornflour	1 teaspoon cornstarch
1 tablespoon paprika pepper	1 tablespoon paprika pepper
2 teaspoons vinegar	2 teaspoons vinegar
1 teaspoon soy sauce	1 teaspoon soy sauce
salt and pepper	salt and pepper
4 hard-boiled eggs, halved	4 hard-cooked eggs, halved
chopped parsley to garnish	chopped parsley for garnish

Melt the butter in a pan and sauté the green pepper, onion and celery for 5 minutes.

Drain the juice from the pineapple and reserve. Add the fruit and tomato purée (paste) to the pan. Blend the cornflour (cornstarch) with the pineapple juice. Stir in the paprika, vinegar and soy sauce. Add to the pan and heat, stirring, until the sauce thickens.

Add salt and pepper to taste and stir in the eggs. Cover and simmer for 5 to 8 minutes. Transfer to a warmed serving dish and garnish with parsley. Serve with rice.
Cooking time: 15 minutes

Soufflé Romantica

METRIC/IMPERIAL	AMERICAN
1 × 310 g/10½ oz can condensed asparagus soup	1 × 10¾ oz can condensed asparagus soup
4 eggs, separated	4 eggs, separated
salt and pepper	salt and pepper

Tie a band of foil around the outside of a greased 900 ml/1½ pint (3¾ cup) soufflé dish to stand 5 cm/2 inches above the rim.

Place the soup in a pan and heat through gently. Beat the egg yolks until thick and creamy, add to the soup and cook for 2 minutes, stirring. Do not allow to boil.

Whisk the egg whites until stiff. Fold a little of the soup mixture into them then add the remainder. Add salt and pepper to taste, then pour into the prepared dish.

Cook the soufflé in a preheated moderately hot oven (190°C/375°F, Gas Mark 5) for 35 minutes until well risen and golden brown. Remove the foil and serve immediately with a green salad.
Cooking time: 40 minutes
Variation:
Condensed mushroom soup can be used in place of the asparagus soup.

Continental Kedgeree

METRIC/IMPERIAL	AMERICAN
3 bratwurst sausages	3 bratwurst sausages
25 g/1 oz butter	2 tablespoons butter
1 tablespoon oil	1 tablespoon oil
1 onion, sliced	1 onion, sliced
1 garlic clove, crushed	1 garlic clove, minced
2 celery sticks, chopped	2 stalks celery, chopped
½ teaspoon turmeric	½ teaspoon turmeric
100 g/4 oz long-grain rice, cooked	½ cup long-grain rice, cooked
salt and pepper	salt and pepper
parsley sprig to garnish	parsley sprig for garnish

Cook the sausages under a preheated moderate grill (broiler) for 8 to 10 minutes on each side until well cooked.

Meanwhile heat the butter and oil in a pan and sauté the onion, garlic and celery for 3 minutes. Stir in the turmeric and rice. Heat gently, stirring, until hot and well blended. Add salt and pepper to taste.

Spoon this mixture into a warmed serving dish. Slice the sausages and arrange around the edge of the rice. Serve with a green salad.
Cooking time: 10 to 15 minutes

Continental Kedgeree
(Photograph: Mattessons Meats)

Spaghetti Provençale

METRIC/IMPERIAL	AMERICAN
2 teaspoons oil	2 teaspoons oil
1 garlic clove, crushed	1 garlic clove, minced
1 onion, chopped	1 onion, chopped
½ green pepper, cored, seeded and chopped	½ green pepper, seeded and chopped
1 small aubergine, chopped	1 small eggplant, chopped
1 × 227 g/8 oz can tomatoes	1 × 8 oz can tomatoes
½ teaspoon dried basil	½ teaspoon dried basil
½ teaspoon dried oregano	½ teaspoon dried oregano
salt and pepper	salt and pepper
100 g/4 oz spaghetti	¼ lb spaghetti
50 g/2 oz Cheddar cheese, grated	½ cup grated Cheddar cheese
25 g/1 oz grated Parmesan cheese	¼ cup grated Parmesan cheese

Heat the oil in a pan and sauté the garlic and onion for 3 minutes. Add the green pepper, aubergine (eggplant), tomatoes, basil and oregano. Add plenty of salt and pepper and bring the vegetable mixture to the boil. Cover and simmer for 30 minutes.

Meanwhile cook the spaghetti in plenty of boiling salted water for 15 minutes or until just soft. Drain and rinse with boiling water. Divide the spaghetti between two warmed serving plates and spoon the vegetables on top. Sprinkle with the Cheddar and Parmesan cheeses. Serve immediately.
Cooking time: 35 minutes

Bacon Toad in the Hole

METRIC/IMPERIAL	AMERICAN
50 g/2 oz plain flour	½ cup all-purpose flour
salt and pepper	salt and pepper
1 egg	1 egg
150 ml/¼ pint milk	⅔ cup milk
4 streaky bacon rashers	4 fatty bacon slices

Sift the flour into a bowl and add salt and pepper. Make a well in the centre and break in the egg. Gradually stir in half the milk. Beat the batter with a wooden spoon until smooth. Stir in the remaining milk.

Remove the rind from the bacon and chop roughly. Place in a roasting tin. Cook the bacon in a preheated moderately hot oven (200°C/400°F, Gas Mark 6) for 5 minutes. Pour over the batter and cook for 20 to 30 minutes until the batter is cooked and well risen. Serve immediately with grilled tomatoes.
Cooking time: 25 to 35 minutes
Variation:
Sausages can be used instead of the bacon, but these should be pre-cooked for 15 minutes before adding the batter.

Potato Bake Special

METRIC/IMPERIAL	AMERICAN
2 large potatoes	2 large potatoes
50 g/2 oz cream cheese	¼ cup cream cheese
garlic granules	garlic granules
salt and pepper	salt and pepper
100 g/4 oz peeled prawns	⅔ cup shelled shrimp

Scrub the potatoes and prick all over with a fork. Cook in a preheated moderately hot oven (190°C/375°F, Gas Mark 5) for 50 minutes to 1 hour or until cooked.

Place the cream cheese in a bowl and soften with a wooden spoon. Stir in the garlic granules and salt and pepper to taste. Add the prawns (shrimp).

Make a crosswise cut in each potato and push in at the base to open. Spoon the cheese mixture on top of the potatoes. Serve immediately wrapped in a napkin.
Cooking time: 50 minutes to 1 hour
Quick Tip:
To make this quicker to prepare, cook extra potatoes (unpeeled) with a main meal and store in the refrigerator. When required, reheat in a moderately hot oven for 20 minutes and continue as in the recipe.

Crispy Tuna

METRIC/IMPERIAL	AMERICAN
1 × 90 g/3½ oz can tuna	1 × 3½ oz can tuna
½ onion, finely chopped	½ onion, finely chopped
25 g/1 oz butter	2 tablespoons butter
25 g/1 oz plain flour	¼ cup all-purpose flour
300 ml/½ pint milk	1¼ cups milk
100 g/4 oz Cheddar cheese, grated	1 cup grated Cheddar cheese
salt and pepper	salt and pepper
2 tomatoes, sliced	2 tomatoes, sliced
50 g/2 oz fresh breadcrumbs	1 cup soft bread crumbs

Drain the oil from the tuna into a small frying pan and sauté the onion until soft. Flake the tuna and place in a greased 600 ml/1 pint (2½ cup) ovenproof dish. Arrange the onion over the top.

Place the butter, flour and milk in a saucepan. Heat, whisking continuously, until the sauce thickens. Continue to cook for 1 minute, then stir in 75 g/3 oz (¾ cup) cheese, and salt and pepper to taste.

Arrange the tomatoes over the tuna and onion then pour over the sauce. Mix the breadcrumbs with the remaining cheese and sprinkle over the top. Place under a preheated, moderate grill (broiler) until golden brown. Serve hot with salad.

Cooking time: 15 to 20 minutes

Variation:

Any canned fish of your choice can be used in place of the tuna.

Quick Fry Supper

METRIC/IMPERIAL	AMERICAN
2 tablespoons oil	2 tablespoons oil
175 g/6 oz ham, diced	¾ cup diced ham
2 tablespoons plain flour	2 tablespoons all-purpose flour
2 tablespoons mild made mustard	2 tablespoons mild prepared mustard
1 tablespoon Worcestershire sauce	1 tablespoon Worcestershire sauce
300 ml/½ pint milk	1¼ cups milk
1 × 283 g/10 oz can green bean chunks, drained	1 × 10 oz can green bean chunks, drained
225 g/8 oz cooked potatoes, sliced	½ lb cooked potatoes, sliced
50 g/2 oz Gruyère cheese, sliced	2 oz Gruyère cheese, sliced
salt and pepper	salt and pepper
green pepper rings to garnish	green pepper rings for garnish

Heat the oil in a pan and fry the ham for 3 minutes. Remove with a slotted spoon and leave on one side. Stir in the flour and cook for 1 minute. Remove pan from heat and gradually add the mustard, Worcestershire sauce and milk. Heat, stirring, until the sauce thickens.

Add the ham, green beans, potatoes and cheese. Heat through gently until the cheese melts. Add salt and pepper to taste. Transfer to two warm serving dishes and garnish with the green pepper rings.

Cooking time: 15 minutes

Main Meals

The recipes in this chapter provide ideas for tasty and tempting main meals. They make good use of chicken, chops and fish to provide fairly quick and nutritious meals for two. Serving suggestions and ideas for accompaniments have been given in many of the recipes.

Cod Catalan

METRIC/IMPERIAL	AMERICAN
25 g/1 oz butter	2 tablespoons butter
onion, sliced	1 onion, sliced
garlic clove, crushed	1 garlic clove, minced
25 g/1 oz plain flour	¼ cup all-purpose flour
1 × 397 g/14 oz can tomatoes	1 × 16 oz can tomatoes
tablespoon tomato purée	1 tablespoon tomato paste
50 g/2 oz stuffed olives, cut in half	⅓ cup halved, stuffed olives
salt and freshly ground black pepper	salt and freshly ground black pepper
2 × 225 g/8 oz cod steaks	2 × ½ lb cod steaks
juice of ½ lemon	juice of ½ lemon
Garnish:	**Garnish:**
25 g/1 oz hazelnuts, chopped	¼ cup chopped hazelnuts
chopped parsley	chopped parsley

Melt the butter in a pan and sauté the onion and garlic until soft. Add the flour and continue to cook for 1 minute. Stir in the tomatoes and the tomato purée (paste). Bring to the boil, stirring, then add the olives and salt and pepper.

Place the cod steaks in a greased shallow ovenproof dish. Sprinkle with the lemon juice and salt and pepper. Pour the tomato sauce over the fish. Cover with foil and cook in a preheated moderate oven (180°C/350°F, Gas Mark 4) for 25 minutes. Serve garnished with the hazelnuts and parsley.
Cooking time: 30 minutes

Cod Catalan
Photograph: Sea Fish Kitchen)

Cider Soused Mackerel

METRIC/IMPERIAL	AMERICAN
2 × 450 g/1 lb whole fresh mackerel	2 × 1 lb whole fresh mackerel
salt and freshly ground black pepper	salt and freshly ground black pepper
½ lemon	½ lemon
1 onion, sliced into rings	1 onion, sliced into rings
sprig of fresh thyme	sprig of fresh thyme
sprig of fresh rosemary	sprig of fresh rosemary
4 bay leaves	4 bay leaves
300 ml/½ pint dry cider	1¼ cups hard cider
150 ml/¼ pint water	⅔ cup water
2 teaspoons arrowroot	2 teaspoons arrowroot

To prepare the mackerel, slit along the belly and remove the guts. Cut off the head and fins and wash well. Season inside the fish with salt and pepper.

Place the fish in a shallow ovenproof dish. Pare the rind from the lemon and place over the mackerel with the onion, herbs and bay leaves. Pour over the cider and all but 1 tablespoon water. Cover the dish with foil and cook in a preheated moderate oven (180°C/350°F, Gas Mark 4) for 30 minutes.

Strain off 300 ml/½ pint of the cooking liquid and reserve. Blend the arrowroot with the remaining tablespoon of water and add to the fish liquid. Place in a pan and heat, stirring, until the sauce thickens and clears. Arrange the fish, onions and herbs on a warmed serving dish and pour over the sauce.
Cooking time: 35 minutes

Mackerel with Almonds

METRIC/IMPERIAL	AMERICAN
2 mackerel fillets	2 mackerel fillets
salt and pepper	salt and pepper
1 lemon, sliced	1 lemon, sliced
1 onion, sliced	1 onion, sliced
15 g/½ oz butter	1 tablespoon butter
25 g/1 oz flaked almonds	¼ cup sliced almonds

Place the mackerel fillets on two pieces of foil. Sprinkle with salt and pepper and cover with lemon and onion slices. Fold the foil over to make two parcels and seal completely. Place on a baking sheet and cook in a preheated, moderately hot oven (200°C/400°F, Gas Mark 6) for 25 minutes.

Melt the butter in a pan and fry the almonds until pale golden brown. Fold back the foil and sprinkle fish with almonds before serving.
Cooking time: 30 minutes

Plaice (Flounder) with Bananas

METRIC/IMPERIAL	AMERICAN
2 streaky bacon rashers	2 fatty bacon slices
25 g/1 oz butter	2 tablespoons butter
2 plaice fillets	2 flounder fillets
salt and freshly ground black pepper	salt and freshly ground black pepper
1 banana	1 banana
Garnish:	**Garnish:**
parsley sprigs	parsley sprigs
lemon wedges	lemon wedges

Remove the rind from the bacon and, on a flat surface, stretch each piece. Cut in half and make four rolls. Cook the bacon rolls under a preheated moderate grill (broiler) until cooked.

Melt 15 g/½ oz (1 tablespoon) butter in the bottom of the grill (broiler) pan, add the fish, skin side down, and cook, basting with the butter from time to time. Sprinkle with salt and pepper to taste.

Melt the remaining butter in a pan. Slice the banana and lightly fry for 5 minutes.

Arrange the fish on a warmed serving dish and top with the bacon rolls and banana. Garnish with parsley and lemon wedges.
Cooking time: 30 minutes

Swirly Fish Pies

METRIC/IMPERIAL	AMERICAN
25 g/1 oz butter	2 tablespoons butter
1 small onion, chopped	1 small onion, chopped
25 g/1 oz plain flour	¼ cup all-purpose flour
300 ml/½ pint milk	1¼ cups milk
50 g/2 oz Cheddar cheese, grated	½ cup grated Cheddar cheese
¼ teaspoon dry mustard	¼ teaspoon dry mustard
salt and pepper	salt and pepper
275 g/10 oz cod, cooked	10 oz cod, cooked
450 g/1 lb potatoes, cooked and mashed	1 lb potatoes, cooked and mashed

Melt the butter in a pan and sauté the onion until soft. Add the flour and continue to cook for 1 minute. Remove from the heat and gradually add the milk. Cook, stirring, until the sauce thickens. Stir in the cheese, mustard and salt and pepper to taste.

Flake the fish and add to the sauce. Spoon into two individual ovenproof dishes.

Place the mashed potato in a piping (pastry) bag fitted with a large fluted nozzle. Starting from the centre, pipe the potato round in circles to cover the pies. Place under a preheated moderate grill (broiler) until golden brown. Serve with a salad.
Cooking time: 20 minutes

Fish Skewers with Nutmeg Rice

METRIC/IMPERIAL	AMERICAN
350 g/12 oz haddock	¾ lb haddock
2 tablespoons vegetable oil	2 tablespoons vegetable oil
salt and freshly ground black pepper	salt and freshly ground black pepper
1 tablespoon lemon juice	1 tablespoon lemon juice
6 bay leaves	6 bay leaves
1 lemon, sliced	1 lemon, sliced
6 stuffed olives	6 stuffed olives
Rice:	**Rice:**
175 g/6 oz long-grain rice	⅞ cup long-grain rice
finely grated rind and juice of ½ lemon	finely grated rind and juice of ½ lemon
15 g/½ oz butter	1 tablespoon butter
½ teaspoon grated nutmeg	½ teaspoon grated nutmeg

Remove any skin and bones from the haddock and cut the fish into cubes. In a bowl, blend together the oil, salt and pepper and lemon juice. Add the fish and leave to marinate for about 30 minutes.

Arrange the fish, bay leaves, lemon slices and olives on two skewers. Brush with the remaining marinade and place under a preheated moderate grill (broiler) for 10 minutes turning several times.

Cook the rice in boiling salted water for 15 minutes or until tender. Drain and rinse. Stir in the lemon rind and juice, butter and nutmeg. Spoon into a hot serving dish and arrange the skewers on top.

Cooking time: 25 minutes

Italian Fish Bake

METRIC/IMPERIAL	AMERICAN
25 g/1 oz butter	2 tablespoons butter
1 garlic clove, crushed	1 garlic clove, minced
225 g/8 oz courgettes, sliced	½ lb zucchini, sliced
1 onion, sliced into rings	1 onion, sliced into rings
½ red pepper, cored, seeded and sliced	½ red pepper, seeded and sliced
½ green pepper, cored, seeded and sliced	½ green pepper, seeded and sliced
100 g/4 oz mushrooms, sliced	1 cup sliced mushrooms
2 × 225 g/8 oz red mullet or snappers	2 × ½ lb snappers
salt and freshly ground black pepper	salt and freshly ground black pepper

Melt the butter in a pan and sauté the garlic, courgettes (zucchini), onion, peppers and mushrooms for 15 minutes.

Using a sharp knife, slit the fish along the belly and remove the guts. Snip off the fins and wash the fish well. Place each fish on a piece of foil and season with salt and pepper.

Arrange the vegetables around each fish, fold over the foil to make two parcels and completely seal. Place the fish parcels on a baking sheet and cook in a preheated moderately hot oven (190°C/375°F, Gas Mark 5) for 30 minutes. Before serving, remove the fish eyes. Arrange the fish on a warmed serving dish with the vegetables. Serve with boiled new potatoes.

Cooking time: 45 minutes

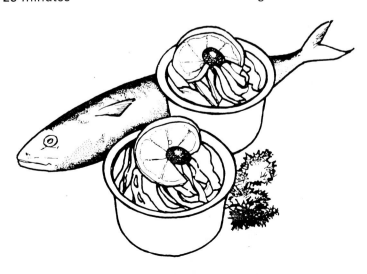

Haddock with Orange Sauce

METRIC/IMPERIAL	AMERICAN
2 × 175 g/6 oz haddock steaks	2 × 6 oz haddock steaks
salt and freshly ground black pepper	salt and freshly ground black pepper
150 ml/¼ pint milk	⅔ cup milk
15 g/½ oz margarine	1 tablespoon margarine
15 g/½ oz plain flour	2 tablespoons all-purpose flour
1 orange	1 orange
parsley sprigs to garnish	parsley sprigs for garnish

Place the haddock in a shallow pan and sprinkle with salt and pepper. Add the milk and cover the pan. Poach for 10 minutes or until the fish is tender. Remove the fish with a slotted spoon and arrange on a serving dish. Keep hot.

Strain off 150 ml/¼ pint (⅔ cup) of the cooking liquid and reserve. Melt the margarine in a pan, add the flour and cook for 1 minute. Remove from the heat and gradually blend in the reserved fish liquid. Heat the sauce, stirring, until it thickens.

Grate the rind from the orange and add to the sauce with salt and pepper to taste. Pour the sauce over the fish.

Remove the skin and pith from the orange and slice the flesh. Garnish the fish with the orange slices and parsley sprigs.

Cooking time: 20 minutes

Tomato Beef Pudding

METRIC/IMPERIAL	AMERICAN
Suet pastry:	**Suet pastry:**
100 g/4 oz self-raising flour	1 cup self-rising flour
50 g/2 oz shredded suet	⅓ cup shredded suet
salt and pepper	salt and pepper
Filling:	**Filling:**
175 g/6 oz minced beef	¾ cup ground beef
1 tablespoon plain flour	1 tablespoon all-purpose flour
salt and pepper	salt and pepper
½ teaspoon dried mixed herbs	½ teaspoon dried mixed herbs
1 × 227 g/8 oz can tomatoes	1 × 8 oz can tomatoes

To make the pastry, mix together the flour, suet and salt and pepper in a bowl. Add sufficient water to make a firm dough.

Roll out two-thirds of the pastry and use to line a 600 ml/1 pint (2½ cup) pudding basin (heatproof mixing bowl).

Mix together the beef, flour, salt and pepper to taste and herbs in a bowl. Spoon into the pastry-lined bowl. Drain the juice from the tomatoes and pour the juice over the meat.

Roll out the remaining pastry to make a lid. Moisten the pastry edges and place the lid in position, sealing the edges well together. Cover the bowl with foil or greaseproof (waxed) paper and secure tightly. Place in a steamer and cook for 2½ to 3 hours.

Turn the pudding on to a warmed serving plate. Break up the tomatoes and heat in a pan then serve as a sauce with the pudding.

Cooking time: about 3 hours

Paprika Beef

METRIC/IMPERIAL	AMERICAN
1 × 425 g/15 oz can stewed steak	1 × 16 oz can stewed steak
1 onion, sliced	1 onion, sliced
1 garlic clove, crushed	1 garlic clove, minced
150 ml/¼ pint beer	⅔ cup beer
2 tablespoons paprika pepper	2 tablespoons paprika pepper
2 tablespoons tomato purée	2 tablespoons tomato paste
1 teaspoon sugar	1 teaspoon sugar
salt and pepper	salt and pepper
175 g/6 oz pasta shells	1½ cups pasta shells
15 g/½ oz butter	1 tablespoon butter
chopped parsley to garnish	chopped parsley for garnish

Turn the contents of the can of stewed steak into a pan and break up with a fork. Add the onion, garlic, beer, paprika, tomato purée (paste), sugar and salt and pepper to taste. Gently bring to the boil, cover and simmer for 20 minutes.

Cook the pasta shells in plenty of boiling salted water for 15 minutes or until tender. Drain and rinse with hot water. Toss the pasta in the butter then arrange it around the edge of a warmed serving dish. Spoon the meat mixture into the centre. Garnish with parsley and serve with a mixed tossed salad.

Cooking time: 35 minutes

Paprika Beef
(Photograph: Canned Food Advisory Bureau)

Chilli Con Carne

METRIC/IMPERIAL	AMERICAN
275 g/10 oz minced beef	1¼ cups ground beef
1 onion, finely chopped	1 onion, finely chopped
½ green pepper, cored, seeded and chopped	½ green pepper, seeded and chopped
1 × 227 g/8 oz can tomatoes	1 × 8 oz can tomatoes
2 tablespoons stock	2 tablespoons stock
½-1 teaspoon chilli powder	½-1 teaspoon chili powder
salt and pepper	salt and pepper
1 × 227 g/8 oz can red kidney beans, drained	1 × 8 oz can red kidney beans, drained
pitta bread to serve	pitta bread to serve

Add the meat to a pan over a moderate heat and fry in its own fat, turning until evenly browned. Add the onion and green pepper and fry for 5 minutes.

Stir in the tomatoes, stock, chilli powder and salt and pepper to taste. Bring to the boil, stirring, cover and simmer for 35 minutes. Add the kidney beans and continue to cook for a further 30 minutes.

Spoon the mixture into two warmed bowls and serve with pitta bread and salad.
Cooking time: 1 hour 10 minutes

Beef Seville

METRIC/IMPERIAL	AMERICAN
25 g/1 oz margarine	2 tablespoons margarine
1 onion, sliced	1 onion, sliced
2 carrots, sliced	2 carrots, sliced
350 g/12 oz chuck steak, cubed	¾ lb chuck steak, cubed
1½ tablespoons plain flour	1½ tablespoons all-purpose flour
grated rind and juice of 1 orange	grated rind and juice of 1 orange
200 ml/⅓ pint beef stock	1 cup beef stock
2 tablespoons orange squash	2 tablespoons orange drink
salt and pepper	salt and pepper
50 g/2 oz dried apricots	⅓ cup dried apricots
watercress to garnish	watercress for garnish

Melt the margarine in a pan and sauté the onion and carrots for 5 minutes. Add the meat and fry, turning, until evenly browned. Sprinkle in the flour and continue to cook for 1 minute. Transfer the meat and vegetables to a 900 ml/1½ pint (3¾ cup) casserole dish.

Stir in the orange rind and juice, stock and orange squash (drink). Add plenty of salt and pepper to taste and the apricots.

Cover and cook in a preheated moderate oven (160°C/325°F, Gas Mark 3) for 1 to 1½ hours. Garnish with watercress and serve with rice or potatoes.
Cooking time: 1 hour 10 minutes to 1 hour 40 minutes

Bacon Steaks with Redcurrant Sauce

METRIC/IMPERIAL	AMERICAN
2 bacon steaks	2 Canadian-style bacon steaks
25 g/1 oz butter, melted	2 tablespoons melted butter
1 dessert apple	1 dessert apple
2 tablespoons redcurrant jelly	2 tablespoons red currant jelly
1 teaspoon wine vinegar	1 teaspoon wine vinegar
1 teaspoon brown sugar	1 teaspoon brown sugar
parsley sprigs to garnish	parsley sprigs for garnish

Snip the fat edges of the steaks to prevent curling. Brush with a little melted butter and place under a preheated moderate grill (broiler) for 5 minutes.

Slice the apple into four rings and remove the core from each. Brush with butter. Turn the bacon steaks over and place the apple rings on top. Continue to grill (broil) for a further 5 minutes, turning the apples once. Transfer to a warmed serving dish and keep hot.

Drain the liquid from the grill (broiler) pan into a saucepan. Add the redcurrant jelly, wine vinegar and brown sugar. Heat gently until the mixture is well blended and slightly syrupy. Spoon the sauce over each bacon steak and garnish with a parsley sprig.
Cooking time: 15 minutes

Spicy Spare Rib Chops

METRIC/IMPERIAL	AMERICAN
350 g/12 oz pork sparerib chops	¾ lb country-style pork ribs
salt	salt
1 onion, sliced	1 onion, sliced
1 garlic clove, crushed	1 garlic clove, minced
1 × 227 g/8 oz can tomatoes	1 × 8 oz can tomatoes
1 teaspoon paprika pepper	1 teaspoon paprika pepper
2 teaspoons Worcestershire sauce	2 teaspoons Worcestershire sauce
1 tablespoon vinegar	1 tablespoon vinegar
1 tablespoon brown sugar	1 tablespoon brown sugar
150 ml/¼ pint dry cider	⅔ cup hard cider
freshly ground black pepper	freshly ground black pepper

Place the pork in the bottom of a greased 1.2 litre/2 pint (5 cup) casserole dish. Sprinkle with salt and cook, uncovered, in a preheated moderately hot oven (200°C/400°F, Gas Mark 6) for 15 minutes.

Place the onion over the pork and continue to cook for 10 minutes.

Combine the garlic, tomatoes, paprika pepper, Worcestershire sauce, vinegar, sugar, cider and salt and pepper to taste, then pour over the pork and onions.

Cover and continue to cook for 45 minutes or until the pork is tender. Serve with jacket potatoes and a green vegetable.
Cooking time: 1 hour 10 minutes

Pork and Bean Casserole

METRIC/IMPERIAL	AMERICAN
2 medium pork sparerib chops	2 medium country-style pork ribs
25 g/1 oz margarine	2 tablespoons margarine
1 small onion, sliced	1 small onion, sliced
2 small carrots, sliced	2 small carrots, sliced
1 medium apple, peeled, cored and sliced	1 medium apple, peeled, cored and sliced
150 ml/¼ pint chicken stock	⅔ cup chicken stock
1 × 210 g/7½ oz can butter beans, drained	1 × 7½ oz can butter beans, drained
sprig of rosemary	sprig of rosemary
½ teaspoon dried thyme	½ teaspoon dried thyme
salt and pepper	salt and pepper
chopped parsley to garnish	chopped parsley for garnish

Cut the meat from the chops (ribs) into cubes. Melt the margarine in a pan and fry the meat until browned all over. Add the onion and carrots and fry gently until soft, then add the apple and cook for 2 minutes.

Stir in the stock, butter beans, rosemary, thyme, salt and pepper to taste. Bring to the boil, cover and simmer for 30 minutes. Adjust the seasoning and transfer to a warmed serving dish. Garnish with parsley and serve with rice and a green salad.
Cooking time: 35 to 40 minutes

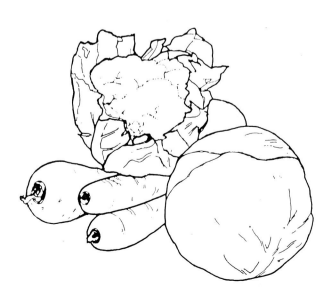

Coconut Rissoles with Curry Rice

METRIC/IMPERIAL	AMERICAN
40 g/1½ oz desiccated coconut	½ cup shredded coconut
225 g/8 oz pork sausagemeat	½ lb pork sausage meat
salt and pepper	salt and pepper
1 egg, beaten	1 egg, beaten
1½ tablespoons oil	1½ tablepoons oil
100 g/4 oz long-grain rice	⅔ cup long-grain rice
1 teaspoon curry powder	1 teaspoon curry powder
300 ml/½ pint water	1¼ cups water
parsley sprigs to garnish	parsley sprigs for garnish

Place the coconut in a bowl and cover with water. Leave to soak for 10 minutes. Squeeze the excess water from the coconut and mix the coconut with the sausagemeat.

Add the salt, pepper and egg, then mix well together. Shape into four rissoles.

Heat 1 tablespoon oil in a frying pan and fry the rissoles for 10 minutes on each side. Drain on kitchen paper towels and keep hot.

Heat the remaining oil in a pan and fry the rice for 1 minute, add the curry powder and continue to cook for 3 minutes. Add the water and some salt. Bring to the boil, stir, cover and simmer for 15 minutes or until the rice is tender and the liquid absorbed.

Arrange the rice and rissoles on a warmed serving dish and garnish with parsley. Serve with a green salad.

Cooking time: 40 minutes

Pork Chops with Piquant Sauce

METRIC/IMPERIAL	AMERICAN
2 pork chops	2 pork chops
15 g/½ oz butter	1 tablespoon butter
1 small onion, chopped	1 small onion, chopped
2 teaspoons plain flour	2 teaspoons all-purpose flour
200 ml/⅓ pint stock	⅞ cup stock
2 teaspoons tomato ketchup	2 teaspoons tomato ketchup
2 teaspoons brown sauce	2 teaspoons brown sauce
2 midget gherkins, sliced	2 midget gherkins, sliced
salt and pepper	salt and pepper

Cook the chops under a preheated moderate grill (broiler) for 15 minutes on each side.

Melt the butter in a pan and sauté the onion for 5 minutes. Stir in the flour and cook for 1 minute. Remove from the heat and gradually add the stock, ketchup and brown sauce. Heat, stirring, until the sauce comes to the boil. Add the gherkins and salt and pepper to taste and heat through for 2 to 3 minutes.

Place the chops on a warmed serving dish and pour over the sauce. Serve with rice and a green vegetable.

Cooking time: 40 minutes

Variation:

Lamb or veal chops can be used as an alternative with the piquant sauce.

Pork Chops with Piquant Sauce
(Photograph: Hammonds Sauce Company)

Mock Chicken Stroganoff

METRIC/IMPERIAL
2 chicken pieces
25 g/1 oz butter
1 onion, sliced
150 ml/¼ pint white
    wine
1 tablespoon milk
1 × 285 g/10 oz can
    mushroom soup
salt and pepper
parsley sprigs to
    garnish

AMERICAN
2 chicken pieces
2 tablespoons butter
1 onion, sliced
⅔ cup white wine
1 tablespoon milk
1 × 10 oz can
    mushroom soup
salt and pepper
parsley sprigs for
    garnish

Cook the chicken pieces under a moderate grill (broiler) for 20 minutes or until they are golden brown all over.

Melt the butter in a pan and sauté the onion until soft. Add the chicken, wine, milk, soup and salt and pepper to taste. Bring to the boil, cover and simmer for 20 minutes or until the chicken is tender. Adjust the seasoning and transfer the chicken to a warmed serving dish. Spoon over the sauce and garnish with parsley sprigs. Serve with noodles or mashed potato.
Cooking time: 50 minutes

Chicken Liver and Aubergine (Eggplant) Casserole

METRIC/IMPERIAL
1 medium aubergine
oil
salt and pepper
50 g/2 oz rice, cooked
2 teaspoons chopped
    parsley
1 medium onion,
    sliced
100 g/4 oz chicken
    livers
3 tablespoons soured
    cream
1 teaspoon paprika
    pepper
2 tomatoes, sliced

AMERICAN
1 medium-size
    eggplant
oil
salt and pepper
¼ cup rice, cooked
2 teaspoons chopped
    parsley
1 medium-size onion,
    sliced
¼ lb chicken livers
3 tablespoons sour
    cream
1 teaspoon paprika
    pepper
2 tomatoes, sliced

Cut the aubergine (eggplant) into 1 cm/½ inch slices. Brush one side of each slice with a little oil. Sprinkle with salt and pepper then cook under a low grill (broiler), without turning, until soft and lightly browned.

Arrange a third of the aubergine (eggplant) slices in the bottom of a 900 ml/1½ pint (3¾ cup) greased casserole dish.

Mix the rice with the parsley and spoon into the dish. Cover with another third of the aubergine (eggplant) slices.

Heat a little oil in a pan and sauté the onion until soft. Add the chicken livers and continue to cook for 4 minutes. Stir in the cream, paprika and salt and pepper to taste. Mix well, then pour into the casserole and top with the remaining aubergine (eggplant) slices.

Arrange the tomato slices around the edge and brush with oil. Cook in a preheated moderately hot oven (200°C/400°F, Gas Mark 6) for 25 to 30 minutes. Serve hot.
Cooking time: 45 minutes

Sweet and Sour Chicken

METRIC/IMPERIAL
oil, for frying
1 teaspoon salt
2 chicken pieces
1 × 297 g/10½ oz can
    sweet and sour
    sauce
1 × 425 g/15 oz can
    apricot halves,
    drained
salt and pepper
25 g/1 oz flaked
    almonds

AMERICAN
oil, for frying
1 teaspoon salt
2 chicken pieces
1 × 10½ can sweet
    and sour sauce
1 × 16 oz can apricot
    halves, drained
salt and pepper
¼ cup sliced almonds

Heat the oil in a frying pan and sprinkle with the salt. Add the chicken pieces and cook for 15 to 20 minutes. Drain well and remove all the flesh from the bone.

Place the sweet and sour sauce in a pan and add the apricots and chicken meat. Add salt and pepper to taste and bring to the boil. Cover and simmer for 10 to 15 minutes.

Meanwhile toast the almonds. Transfer the chicken to a warmed serving dish and sprinkle with the almonds. Serve with boiled rice and stir-fried vegetables.
Cooking time: 30 minutes

Chicken Noodle Moussaka

METRIC/IMPERIAL
100 g/4 oz pasta
    noodles
1 aubergine
25 g/1 oz margarine
½ green pepper,
    cored, seeded and
    chopped
1 small onion,
    chopped
1 garlic clove, crushed
2 tomatoes, skinned
    and chopped
100 g/4 oz cooked
    chicken meat,
    chopped
salt and pepper
chopped parsley to
    garnish
Sauce:
15 g/½ oz margarine
15 g/½ oz plain flour
250 ml/8 fl oz chicken
    stock
1 egg yolk
Topping:
2 tablespoons fresh
    breadcrumbs
15 g/½ oz margarine

AMERICAN
1 cup pasta noodles
1 eggplant
2 tablespoons
    margarine
½ green pepper,
    seeded and
    chopped
1 small onion,
    chopped
1 garlic clove, minced
2 tomatoes, peeled
    and chopped
½ cup chopped
    cooked chicken
    meat
salt and pepper
chopped parsley for
    garnish
Sauce:
1 tablespoon
    margarine
2 tablespoons
    all-purpose flour
1 cup chicken stock
1 egg yolk
Topping:
2 tablespoons soft
    bread crumbs
1 tablespoon
    margarine

Cook the noodles in plenty of boiling salted water for 15 minutes or until they are soft. Drain and rinse.

Slice the aubergine (eggplant), place in a colander and sprinkle with salt; leave for 30 minutes. Melt 15 g/½ oz (1 tablespoon) of the margarine in a pan and sauté the aubergine (eggplant) slices until soft. Remove and leave on one side.

Melt the remaining margarine in the pan and sauté the green pepper, onion and garlic until soft. Add the tomatoes, chicken and salt and pepper to taste.

Arrange layers of noodles, aubergine (eggplant) and chicken mixture in a greased 1.2 litre/2 pint (5 cup) ovenproof dish.

To make the sauce, place the margarine, flour and stock in a pan and whisk over a moderate heat until the sauce thickens. Continue to cook the sauce, stirring, for 1 minute. Cool slightly and beat in the egg yolk.

Pour the sauce over the layers in the dish.

Sprinkle with the breadcrumbs and dot with the margarine. Cook in a preheated moderate oven (180°C/350°F, Gas Mark 4) for 40 minutes.
Cooking time: 1 hour 10 minutes

Chicken with Peaches

METRIC/IMPERIAL
25 g/1 oz margarine
2 chicken pieces
1 onion, chopped
1 green pepper,
    cored, seeded and
    sliced
1 teaspoon ground
    cinnamon
½ × 283 g/10 oz can
    peach slices
1 teaspoon cornflour
150 ml/¼ pint stock
salt and pepper
watercress to garnish

AMERICAN
2 tablespoons
    margarine
2 chicken pieces
1 onion, chopped
1 green pepper,
    seeded and sliced
1 teaspoon ground
    cinnamon
½ × 10 oz can peach
    slices
1 teaspoon cornstarch
⅔ cup stock
salt and pepper
watercress for
    garnish

Melt the margarine in a pan and fry the chicken for 15 minutes, turning frequently; remove from the pan. Add the onion, green pepper and cinnamon to the pan and sauté until soft.

Drain the juice from the peaches and reserve. Blend 1 tablespoon of the juice with the cornflour (cornstarch). Add the remaining juice to the pan with the stock, chicken and salt and pepper to taste. Bring to the boil, cover and simmer for 10 minutes. Add the peaches and the blended cornflour (cornstarch). Continue to cook for 10 minutes.

Transfer to a warmed serving dish and garnish with watercress.
Cooking time: 40 minutes

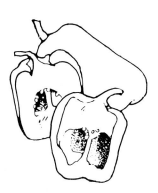

Chicken à la Maize

METRIC/IMPERIAL	AMERICAN
2 chicken pieces	2 chicken pieces
6 peppercorns	6 peppercorns
1 bay leaf	1 bay leaf
sprig of thyme	sprig of thyme
15 g/½ oz butter	1 tablespoon butter
50 g/2 oz mushrooms, sliced	½ cup sliced mushrooms
1 stock cube	2 bouillon cubes
25 g/1 oz margarine	2 tablespoons margarine
25 g/1 oz plain flour	¼ cup all-purpose flour
salt and pepper	salt and pepper
1 × 198 g/7 oz can sweetcorn	1 × 7 oz can whole kernel corn
watercress to garnish	watercress for garnish

Place the chicken pieces in a pan and cover with water. Add the peppercorns, bay leaf and thyme. Bring to the boil, cover and simmer for 30 minutes or until the chicken is tender.

Melt the butter in a pan and lightly sauté the mushrooms. Remove the mushrooms and leave on one side.

Remove the chicken and keep hot. Strain off 300 ml/½ pint (1¼ cups) of the stock and stir in the stock (bouillon) cube.

Melt the margarine in a pan and stir in the flour. Cook for 1 minute or until a pale golden colour. Remove from the heat and gradually blend in the stock. Heat, stirring, until the sauce thickens and continue to cook for 1 minute. Add salt and pepper to taste and then stir in the cooked mushrooms.

Heat the corn and drain. Arrange the chicken on a warmed serving dish and pour over the sauce. Spoon the corn around the chicken and garnish with watercress.

Cooking time: 45 to 50 minutes

Spiced Citrus Bake

METRIC/IMPERIAL	AMERICAN
1 orange, sliced	1 orange, sliced
2 lamb leg bone steaks	2 lamb leg bone steaks
salt and pepper	salt and pepper
¼ teaspoon ground ginger	¼ teaspoon ground ginger
1 teaspoon brown sugar	1 teaspoon brown sugar
½ lemon, sliced	½ lemon, sliced
150 ml/¼ pint stock	⅔ cup stock
1 teaspoon cornflour	1 teaspoon cornstarch
1 tablespoon water	1 tablespoon water
parsley sprigs to garnish	parsley sprigs for garnish

Cover the bottom of a small roasting dish with the orange slices. Sprinkle the lamb steaks with salt and pepper and place on top.

Mix together the ginger and sugar, then sprinkle over the lamb. Place a slice of lemon on each lamb steak and pour over the stock.

Cook, uncovered, in a preheated moderate oven (180°C/350°F, Gas Mark 4) for 1 hour.

Blend the cornflour (cornstarch) with the water. Drain the juices from the lamb and pour on to the cornflour (cornstarch) mixture. Pour into a saucepan and heat, stirring, until the sauce has thickened.

Arrange the lamb on a warmed serving dish and pour over the sauce. Garnish with the orange and lemon slices and parsley sprigs.

Cooking time: 1 hour 5 minutes

Spiced Citrus Bake
(Photograph: New Zealand Lamb Information Bureau)

Malayan Curry

METRIC/IMPERIAL
1 tablespoon oil
275 g/10 oz stewing
  lamb, cut into
  cubes
1 onion, chopped
2 teaspoons curry
  powder
½ teaspoon ground
  cinnamon
pinch of cayenne
  pepper
salt and pepper
200 ml/⅓ pint stock
1 dessert apple,
  peeled, cored and
  chopped
1 tablespoon
  desiccated coconut
150 g/5 oz long grain
  rice

AMERICAN
1 tablespoon oil
1½ cups cubed
  boneless lamb for
  stew
1 onion, chopped
2 teaspoons curry
  powder
½ teaspoon ground
  cinnamon
pinch of cayenne
  pepper
salt and pepper
⅞ cup stock
1 dessert apple,
  peeled, cored and
  chopped
1 tablespoon
  shredded coconut
¾ cup long grain rice

Heat the oil in a pan and fry the meat until browned all over. Add the onion and continue to cook for 2 minutes.

Stir in the curry powder, cinnamon, cayenne pepper and salt and pepper to taste. Continue to cook for 1 minute. Add the stock, apple and coconut. Bring to the boil, cover and simmer for 1½ hours. Stir occasionally and add more liquid if necessary.

Cook the rice in plenty of boiling salted water for 15 minutes or until tender. Drain and rinse.

Arrange the rice around the edge of a warmed serving dish and spoon the curry into the centre.
Cooking time: 1 hour 35 minutes

Lamb Cutlets with Lemon Rice

METRIC/IMPERIAL
150 g/5 oz long grain
  rice
salt and freshly
  ground black
  pepper
1 lemon
1 garlic clove, crushed
2 lamb cutlets
1 tablespoon oil
Garnish:
watercress
tomato slices

AMERICAN
¾ cup long grain rice
salt and freshly
  ground black
  pepper
1 lemon
1 garlic clove, minced
2 rib lamb chops
1 tablespoon oil
Garnish:
watercress
tomato slices

Cook the rice in plenty of boiling salted water adding a piece of lemon peel.

Meanwhile rub the garlic into the lamb, sprinkle with salt and pepper and brush with oil. Cook under a preheated moderate grill (broiler) for 15 minutes, turning once.

Grate the rind from the lemon and squeeze the juice. Drain the rice, rinse with hot water and drain. Stir in the lemon rind, juice and salt and pepper to taste. Spoon into a warmed serving dish and arrange the lamb on top. Garnish with watercress and tomato slices.
Cooking time: 30 minutes

Kidney Kebabs with Barbecue Sauce

METRIC/IMPERIAL	AMERICAN
4 small onions	4 small onions
4 streaky bacon rashers	4 fatty bacon slices
4 lambs' kidneys	4 lamb kidneys
2 chipolata sausages, halved	2 small sausages, halved
Baste:	**Baste:**
1 teaspoon tomato purée	1 teaspoon tomato paste
1 teaspoon Worcestershire sauce	1 teaspoon Worcestershire sauce
2 teaspoons oil	2 teaspoons oil
Sauce:	**Sauce:**
15 g/½ oz margarine	1 tablespoon margarine
½ small onion, finely chopped	½ small onion, minced
4 tablespoons tomato ketchup	4 tablespoons tomato ketchup
4 tablespoons Worcestershire sauce	4 tablespoons Worcestershire sauce
1 tablespoon clear honey	1 tablespoon honey
1 tablespoon lemon juice	1 tablespoon lemon juice
salt and pepper	salt and pepper

Cook the onions in boiling salted water for 5 minutes, then drain. Remove the rind from the bacon, stretch each rasher (slice) on a board with the back of a knife, then cut in half. Roll up each piece of bacon. Halve the kidneys and remove the cores.

Thread the onions, bacon, kidneys and sausages onto two skewers. Mix the baste ingredients together and brush over the kebabs. Cook under a preheated moderate grill (broiler) for 5 minutes on each side. Brush with any extra baste while cooking.

To make the sauce, melt the margarine in a pan and gently sauté the onion for 5 minutes. Add the tomato ketchup, Worcestershire sauce, honey, lemon juice and salt and pepper to taste. Bring to the boil and then simmer for 5 minutes.

Arrange the kebabs on a bed of rice and serve with the sauce.
Cooking time: 25 to 30 minutes

Crispy Topped Liver

METRIC/IMPERIAL	AMERICAN
25 g/1 oz margarine	2 tablespoons margarine
225 g/8 oz lambs' liver, sliced	½ lb lamb liver, sliced
1 small onion, chopped	1 small onion, chopped
50 g/2 oz mushrooms, chopped	½ cup chopped mushrooms
½ red pepper, cored, seeded and chopped	½ red pepper, seeded and chopped
40 g/1½ oz fresh breadcrumbs	¾ cup soft bread crumbs
1 teaspoon dried mixed herbs	1 teaspoon dried mixed herbs
1 egg, beaten	1 egg, beaten
salt and pepper	salt and pepper
parsley sprigs to garnish	parsley sprigs for garnish

Melt the margarine in a frying pan and fry the liver for 15 minutes, turning once. Remove from the pan with a slotted spoon and keep hot in an ovenproof dish.

Add the onion, mushrooms and red pepper to the pan and sauté for 3 minutes. Stir in the breadcrumbs, herbs, beaten egg and salt and pepper to taste. Continue to cook, stirring, for 2 minutes. Spoon the mixture over the liver and cook under a preheated moderate grill (broiler) for 3 to 5 minutes until the topping is crisp and golden brown.

Serve hot, garnished with parsley sprigs.
Cooking time: 25 minutes

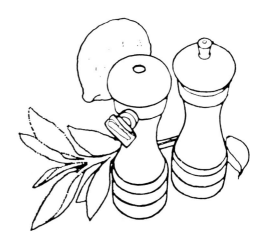

Salads and Vegetable Dishes

Many of these salads are substantial enough for a meal and they make good use of leftover cooked foods and vegetables in season. Some of the vegetable dishes can be served as light meals such as Stuffed Peppers, Broccoli Bake and Trio Bean Bake. Others make good accompaniments to simple meat, poultry and fish dishes.

Chicory and Potato Salad

METRIC/IMPERIAL	AMERICAN
1 medium head of chicory	1 medium head of endive
1 × 283 g/10 oz carton potato salad	1 × 10 oz carton potato salad
1 × 75 g/3½ oz can tuna fish, drained	1 × 3½ oz can tuna fish, drained
100 g/4 oz French beans, sliced and cooked	¼ lb green beans, sliced and cooked
2 tomatoes, quartered	2 tomatoes, quartered
10 black olives	10 ripe olives
chopped parsley to garnish	chopped parsley for garnish

Separate the chicory (endive) leaves and arrange around the edge of a serving plate. Spoon the potato salad into the middle. Mix together the tuna, beans, tomatoes and olives and arrange around the edge of the potato.

Garnish with chopped parsley and serve with French bread.

Tasty Sausage Salad

METRIC/IMPERIAL	AMERICAN
225 g/8 oz sausages, cooked and sliced	½ lb sausages, cooked and sliced
3 spring onions, chopped	3 scallions, chopped
50 g/2 oz cooked peas	½ cup cooked peas
1 small banana, sliced	1 small banana, sliced
1 small dessert apple, cored and chopped	1 small apple, cored and chopped
lemon juice	lemon juice
1 orange, peeled and segmented	1 orange, peeled and segmented
25 g/1 oz seedless raisins	3 tablespoons seedless raisins
4 tablespoons plain yogurt	4 tablespoons plain yogurt
salt and pepper	salt and pepper
few lettuce leaves	few lettuce leaves

Place the sausages in a bowl and add the spring onions (scallions) and peas. Dip the banana and apple in lemon juice and add to the bowl with the orange and raisins.

Stir in the yogurt and mix well. Add salt and pepper to taste.

Arrange the lettuce on a serving dish and spoon the salad mixture on top. Serve with crusty bread or rolls.

Chicory and Potato Salad
(Photograph: Mattessons Meats)

35

Sardine Salad

METRIC/IMPERIAL
100 g/4 oz white
  cabbage, shredded
2 celery sticks,
  chopped
1 red dessert apple,
  cored and chopped
½ small onion,
  chopped
1 carrot, grated
3 tablespoons salad
  cream
salt and pepper
1 × 125 g/4¼ oz can
  sardines
2 tablespoons soured
  cream

AMERICAN
1½ cups shredded
  white cabbage
2 stalks celery,
  chopped
1 red-skinned dessert
  apple, cored and
  chopped
½ small onion,
  chopped
1 carrot, grated
3 tablespoons salad
  cream
salt and pepper
1 × 4¼ oz can
  sardines
2 tablespoons sour
  cream

Place the cabbage in a bowl with the celery, apple, onion and carrot. Stir in the salad cream and add salt and pepper to taste.

Arrange the salad in a shallow serving dish. Drain the oil from the sardines and arrange them on top of the salad. Spoon over the sour cream and serve with wholewheat bread.

Avocado and Corn

METRIC/IMPERIAL
1 avocado
1 teaspoon sugar
1 teaspoon
  mayonnaise
1 × 198 g/7 oz can
  sweetcorn, drained
1 dessert pear,
  peeled, cored and
  grated
50 g/2 oz ham, finely
  chopped
salt and pepper

AMERICAN
1 avocado
1 teaspoon sugar
1 teaspoon
  mayonnaise
1 × 7 oz can whole
  kernel corn, drained
1 dessert pear,
  peeled, cored and
  grated
¼ cup finely chopped
  ham
salt and pepper

Cut the avocado in half lengthwise, remove the stone (seed) and scoop out the flesh. Place in a bowl with the sugar and mayonnaise and mash together with a fork.

Stir in half the sweetcorn, the pear and ham. Add salt and pepper to taste. Pile the mixture back into the avocado halves. Place on two serving dishes and arrange the remaining corn around the edge. Serve with thinly sliced brown bread and butter.

Lazy Pineapple Salad

METRIC/IMPERIAL
225 g/8 oz cottage
  cheese
25 g/1 oz walnuts,
  chopped
25 g/1 oz sultanas
salt and pepper
bunch of watercress
2 slices pineapple
cucumber slices
parsley sprigs to
  garnish

AMERICAN
1 cup cottage cheese
¼ cup chopped
  walnuts
3 tablespoons
  seedless raisins
salt and pepper
bunch of watercress
2 slices pineapple
cucumber slices
parsley sprigs for
  garnish

Place the cottage cheese in a bowl and add the walnuts, sultanas (raisins) and salt and pepper to taste.

Arrange the watercress around the edge of two serving plates. Place a pineapple slice in the centre and spoon the cottage cheese mixture on top. Arrange the cucumber slices around the edge and garnish each dish with parsley sprigs.

Prawn and Melon Salad Cocktails

METRIC/IMPERIAL	AMERICAN
1 small melon	1 small melon
50 g/2 oz peeled prawns	1/3 cup shelled shrimp
1 teaspoon capers	1 teaspoon capers
1 celery stick, finely chopped	1 stalk celery, minced
2 tablespoons mayonnaise	2 tablespoons mayonnaise
2 teaspoons tomato purée	2 teaspoons tomato paste
1/2 teaspoon Worcestershire sauce	1/2 teaspoon Worcestershire sauce
salt and pepper	salt and pepper
Garnish:	**Garnish:**
chopped parsley	chopped parsley
2 unpeeled prawns	2 unshelled shrimp

Cut the melon in half and remove the seeds. Chill the melon.

Mix together the prawns (shrimp), capers and celery. Combine the mayonnaise, tomato purée (paste), Worcestershire sauce and salt and pepper to taste. Stir the prawn (shrimp) mixture into the dressing.

Just before serving, spoon the mixture into the melon halves. Place on two serving plates and garnish with chopped parsley and the whole prawns. Serve with thinly sliced brown bread and butter.

Edam and Banana Salad

METRIC/IMPERIAL	AMERICAN
few lettuce leaves	few lettuce leaves
175 g/6 oz Edam cheese, cubed	1 cup diced Edam cheese
1 dessert apple, cored and diced	1 apple, cored and diced
1 small red pepper, cored, seeded and chopped	1 small red pepper, seeded and chopped
1 celery stick, chopped	1 stalk celery, chopped
2 bananas, sliced	2 bananas, sliced
lemon juice	lemon juice
salt and pepper	salt and pepper
chopped parsley to garnish	chopped parsley for garnish
French dressing (optional)	vinaigrette dressing (optional)

Arrange the lettuce leaves on a serving dish.

Place the cheese in a bowl with the apple, red pepper and celery. Dip the banana slices in lemon juice and add to the other ingredients. Mix well and add salt and pepper to taste.

Spoon onto the lettuce and garnish with parsley. Serve with French (vinaigrette) dressing if liked.

Store Cupboard Salad

METRIC/IMPERIAL	AMERICAN
100 g/4 oz long grain rice, cooked	½ cup long grain rice, cooked
3 tablespoons canned sweetcorn	3 tablespoons canned whole kernel corn
25 g/1 oz unsalted peanuts	2 tablespoons unsalted peanuts
3 frankfurters, cooked	3 frankfurters, cooked
1 dessert apple, cored and chopped	1 dessert apple, cored and chopped
lemon juice	lemon juice
3 tablespoons French dressing	3 tablespoons vinaigrette dressing
salt and pepper	salt and pepper

Place the rice in a bowl and add the corn and peanuts. Slice the frankfurters and add to the bowl. Mix the apple with some lemon juice and stir into the rice mixture with the French (vinaigrette) dressing. Mix well and add salt and pepper to taste. Spoon into a serving dish.

Avocado and Apple Salad

METRIC/IMPERIAL	AMERICAN
1 red dessert apple	1 red-skinned dessert apple
1 tablespoon raisins	1 tablespoon raisins
1 tablespoon chopped nuts	1 tablespoon chopped nuts
2 celery sticks, chopped	2 stalks celery, chopped
2 tablespoons mayonnaise	2 tablespoons mayonnaise
1 avocado	1 avocado
salt and pepper	salt and pepper

Core and dice the apple. Mix with the raisins, chopped nuts and celery. Add the mayonnaise and toss lightly.

Just before serving, halve, peel and remove the stone (seed) from the avocado. Cut into dice and mix into the salad. Add salt and pepper to taste. Serve as a starter or side salad.

Vegetable Soup

METRIC/IMPERIAL	AMERICAN
1 leek	1 leek
25 g/1 oz butter	2 tablespoons butter
1 celery stick, chopped	1 stalk celery, chopped
1 large potato, peeled and sliced	1 large potato, peeled and sliced
1 carrot, grated	1 carrot, grated
300 ml/½ pint chicken stock	1¼ cups chicken stock
150 ml/¼ pint dry cider	⅔ cup hard cider
salt and pepper	salt and pepper

Slice the leek into 1 cm/½ inch pieces. Melt the butter in a pan and add the leek. Cover and sauté gently for 1 minute.

Add the celery and potato and continue to sauté gently for 5 minutes. Add the carrot, stock, cider and salt and pepper to taste. Bring to the boil, cover and simmer for 40 minutes until all the vegetables are tender. Check the seasoning and serve hot with grated cheese and wholewheat bread.

Cooking time: 45 minutes

Variation:

Any vegetables in season can be added to the soup: e.g. cauliflower, swede (rutabaga), onions, green beans, courgettes (zucchini).

Vegetable Soup
(Photograph: Woodstock saucepan from
Pointerware [UK] Ltd)

Chicken Fruit Salad

METRIC/IMPERIAL
½ honeydew melon
1 pear, cored and
    chopped
50 g/2 oz seedless
    green grapes
25 g/1 oz stoned
    dates, chopped
50 g/2 oz walnuts,
    chopped
225 g/8 oz cooked
    chicken, cut into
    strips
2 tablespoons
    mayonnaise
2 tablespoons plain
    yogurt
salt and pepper
chopped parsley to
    garnish

AMERICAN
½ honeydew melon
1 pear, cored and
    chopped
½ cup seedless white
    grapes
3 tablespoons pitted
    and chopped dates
½ cup chopped
    walnuts
½ lb cooked chicken,
    cut into strips
2 tablespoons
    mayonnaise
2 tablespoons plain
    yogurt
salt and pepper
chopped parsley for
    garnish

Remove the seeds from the melon. Scoop out the flesh and cut into dice. Place in a bowl with the pear, grapes, dates and walnuts.

Add the chicken to the fruit with the mayonnaise and yogurt. Mix well and add salt and pepper to taste. Spoon into a serving dish and garnish with chopped parsley.

Minted Melon and Strawberry Cocktail

METRIC/IMPERIAL
1 Ogen melon
50 g/2 oz strawberries,
    hulled and sliced
5 cm/2 inch piece
    cucumber, sliced
    and quartered
finely grated rind and
    juice of 1 small
    orange
1 tablespoon chopped
    mint
a few lettuce leaves
2 mint sprigs to
    garnish

AMERICAN
1 Ogen melon
½ cup hulled and
    sliced strawberries
2 inch piece
    cucumber, sliced
    and quartered
finely grated rind and
    juice of 1 small
    orange
1 tablespoon chopped
    mint
a few lettuce leaves
2 mint sprigs for
    garnish

Cut the melon in half and discard the seeds. Cut the flesh into 1 cm/½ inch cubes or scoop into balls. Place the melon in a bowl with the strawberries and cucumber.

Mix the orange rind and juice with the chopped mint, then pour onto the salad and mix gently together.

Shred the lettuce and use to line the melon shells. Spoon the salad on top, pouring in any orange juice from the bowl. Serve chilled as an appetizer, garnished with sprigs of mint.

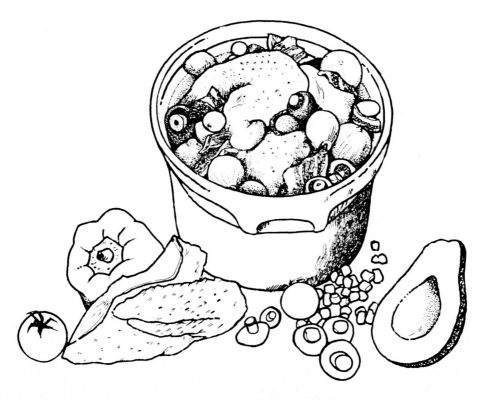

Trio Bean Bake

METRIC/IMPERIAL	AMERICAN
50 g/2 oz dried chick peas	⅓ cup dried chick peas
50 g/2 oz dried butter beans	⅓ cup dried butter beans
50 g/2 oz dried red kidney beans	⅓ cup dried red kidney beans
1 garlic clove, crushed	1 garlic clove, minced
1 onion, chopped	1 onion, chopped
1 × 396 g/14 oz can tomatoes	1 × 16 oz can tomatoes
1 green pepper, cored, seeded and chopped	1 green pepper, seeded and chopped
½ teaspoon ground ginger	½ teaspoon ground ginger
¼ teaspoon ground cloves	¼ teaspoon ground cloves
150 ml/¼ pint stock	⅔ cup stock
salt and pepper	salt and pepper
chopped parsley to garnish	chopped parsley for garnish

Place the chick peas, butter beans and kidney beans in a bowl and cover with cold water. Leave to soak overnight.

Drain the peas and beans, then place them in a pan and cover with fresh cold water. Bring to the boil, boil for 10 minutes then simmer for 40 to 45 minutes or until tender. Drain and rinse under cold water.

Return the beans to the pan and add the garlic, onion, tomatoes, green pepper, ginger, cloves, stock and salt and pepper to taste. Bring to the boil, cover and simmer for 1 hour, adding water if the mixture becomes too dry. Check the seasoning, then transfer to a warmed serving dish. Garnish with parsley. Serve with cheese and crusty rolls, bacon chops, sausages or beefburgers.

Cooking time: 1 hour 55 minutes

Rice Salad with Apple and Nuts

METRIC/IMPERIAL	AMERICAN
100 g/4 oz long grain rice	½ cup long grain rice
300 ml/½ pint water	1¼ cups water
1 teaspoon salt	1 teaspoon salt
2 dessert apples, cored and chopped	2 dessert apples, cored and chopped
40 g/1½ oz mixed nuts, chopped	⅓ cup chopped mixed nuts
75 g/3 oz cooked ham, diced	⅓ cup diced cooked ham
Dressing:	**Dressing:**
2 tablespoons vinegar	2 tablespoons vinegar
2 tablespoons olive oil	2 tablespoons olive oil
salt and pepper	salt and pepper
½ teaspoon sugar	½ teaspoon sugar

Place the rice, water and salt in a pan. Bring to the boil and stir once. Cover and simmer for 15 minutes or until the rice is tender and the liquid absorbed. Leave to cool in a bowl.

Add the apple, nuts and ham to the rice and toss together. Place the dressing ingredients in a screw top jar and shake until well blended. Pour over the salad and mix well. Transfer to a serving bowl.

Cooking time: 15 to 20 minutes

Stuffed Cabbage Leaves with Cider

METRIC/IMPERIAL
4 large green cabbage
  leaves
salt and pepper
75 g/3 oz liver
  sausage
75 g/3 oz
  sausagemeat
25 g/1 oz fresh
  breadcrumbs
2 teaspoons chopped
  parsley
½ teaspoon dried
  mixed herbs
15 g/½ oz margarine
1 small onion,
  chopped
½ small cooking
  apple, peeled,
  cored and chopped
1 tablespoon plain
  flour
4 tablespoons chicken
  stock
150 ml/¼ pint dry
  cider

AMERICAN
4 large green cabbage
  leaves
salt and pepper
⅓ cup liver sausage
⅓ cup sausage meat
½ cup soft bread
  crumbs
2 teaspoons chopped
  parsley
½ teaspoon dried
  mixed herbs
1 tablespoon
  margarine
1 small onion,
  chopped
½ small tart apple,
  peeled, cored and
  chopped
1 tablespoon
  all-purpose flour
4 tablespoons chicken
  stock
⅔ cup hard cider

Trim the cabbage leaves and cook in boiling salted water for 2 minutes. Drain and cool.

In a bowl, mix together the liver sausage, sausagemeat, breadcrumbs, parsley, herbs and salt and pepper to taste. Blend well and divide the mixture between the cabbage leaves. Roll up, turning the ends in to make neat parcels. Arrange in a greased, shallow ovenproof dish.

Melt the margarine in a pan and sauté the onion and apple for 3 minutes. Stir in the flour and continue to cook for 1 minute. Remove from the heat and gradually blend in the stock and cider. Heat, stirring, until the mixture thickens. Add salt and pepper to taste, then pour the sauce over the cabbage parcels.

Cover the dish with foil and cook in a preheated moderate oven (180°C/350°F, Gas Mark 4) for 45 minutes. Serve hot with boiled potatoes and grilled tomatoes.
Cooking time: 55 minutes

Tomato and Olive Rice

METRIC/IMPERIAL
1 tablespoon oil
1 onion, chopped
1 garlic clove,
  crushed
100 g/4 oz long grain
  rice
6 tomatoes, skinned
  and quartered
300 ml/½ pint chicken
  stock
salt and pepper
finely grated rind of
  ½ lemon
2 sprigs fresh
  rosemary, chopped
  or 1 teaspoon dried
  rosemary
75 g/3 oz stuffed
  olives, sliced
lemon slices to
  garnish

AMERICAN
1 tablespoon oil
1 onion, chopped
1 garlic clove, minced
½ cup long grain rice
6 tomatoes, peeled
  and quartered
1¼ cups chicken
  stock
salt and pepper
finely grated rind of
  ½ lemon
2 sprigs fresh
  rosemary, chopped
  or 1 teaspoon dried
  rosemary
½ cup sliced stuffed
  olives
lemon slices for
  garnish

Heat the oil in a pan and sauté the onion and garlic for 3 minutes. Add the rice and continue to fry for 2 minutes.

Add the tomatoes, stock, salt and pepper, lemon rind and rosemary. Bring to the boil, cover and simmer for 15 to 20 minutes until the rice is cooked and the liquid absorbed. Stir in the olives, check the seasoning and garnish with lemon slices. Serve with meat or fish.
Cooking time: 20 to 25 minutes

Tomato and Olive Rice
(Photograph: Rice Council)

Broccoli Bake

METRIC/IMPERIAL
350 g/12 oz fresh or
    frozen broccoli
salt and pepper
2 tomatoes, quartered
25 g/1 oz dry
    breadcrumbs
Sauce:
25 g/1 oz butter
25 g/1 oz plain flour
300 ml/½ pint milk
75 g/3 oz cheese,
    grated
½ teaspoon made
    mustard

AMERICAN
¾ lb fresh or frozen
    broccoli
salt and pepper
2 tomatoes, quartered
¼ cup dry bread
    crumbs
Sauce:
2 tablespoons butter
¼ cup all-purpose
    flour
1¼ cups milk
¾ cup grated cheese
½ teaspoon prepared
    mustard

Cook the broccoli in boiling salted water for 5 to 8 minutes. Drain and arrange in a greased, shallow ovenproof dish.

To make the sauce, melt the butter in a pan, stir in the flour and cook for 1 minute. Remove from the heat and gradually blend in the milk. Heat, stirring, until the sauce thickens. Stir in the grated cheese, mustard and salt and pepper to taste.

Pour the sauce over the broccoli, arrange the tomatoes around the edge and sprinkle with breadcrumbs. Cook in a preheated moderately hot oven (200°C/400°F, Gas Mark 6) for 15 minutes until golden brown. Serve hot.
Cooking time: 30 minutes

Highland Mushrooms

METRIC/IMPERIAL
50 g/2 oz butter
225 g/8 oz button
    mushrooms,
    quartered
4 tablespoons whisky
15 g/½ oz stem
    ginger, cut into dice
150 ml/¼ pint single
    cream
1 tablespoon
    cornflour
salt and freshly
    ground black
    pepper
parsley sprigs to
    garnish

AMERICAN
¼ cup butter
2 cups quartered
    mushrooms
4 tablespoons whisky
1 tablespoon chopped
    preserved ginger
⅔ cup light cream
1 tablespoon
    cornstarch
salt and freshly
    ground black
    pepper
parsley sprigs for
    garnish

Melt the butter in a pan and lightly sauté the mushrooms for 2 to 3 minutes. Stir in the whisky and ginger.

Blend the cream with the cornflour (cornstarch) and stir into the mushrooms. Heat gently, stirring, until the mixture thickens but do not allow to boil. Add a little salt and pepper to taste.

Serve immediately as an accompaniment to meat or on toast as a snack or starter. Garnish with parsley sprigs.
Cooking time: 8 to 10 minutes

Stuffed Peppers

METRIC/IMPERIAL	AMERICAN
green peppers	2 green peppers
tomatoes, skinned and chopped	2 tomatoes, peeled and chopped
0 g/2 oz fresh breadcrumbs	1 cup soft bread crumbs
½ dessert apple, cored and chopped	½ dessert apple, cored and chopped
0 g/2 oz Edam cheese, finely grated	½ cup finely grated Edam cheese
0 g/1½ oz garlic sausage, finely chopped	2 tablespoons finely chopped garlic sausage
½ teaspoon French mustard	½ teaspoon Dijon-style mustard
alt and pepper	salt and pepper

ut the tops off the peppers and reserve; dis-
ard the seeds and cores. Blanch in boiling
alted water for 2 minutes, then drain.

Place the tomatoes in a bowl with the
readcrumbs, apple, cheese, garlic sausage,
ustard and salt and pepper to taste. Mix well
nd spoon the mixture into the peppers.

Replace the lids and place in a shallow
venproof dish. Cook in a preheated
oderately hot oven (190°C/375°F, Gas Mark 5)
r 20 minutes. Serve hot as a starter or with
old meats and salad.
ooking time: 20 minutes

Celery in Grapefruit Sauce

METRIC/IMPERIAL	AMERICAN
head celery	1 bunch celery
alt and pepper	salt and pepper
5 g/½ oz margarine	1 tablespoon margarine
5 g/½ oz plain flour	2 tablespoons all-purpose flour
50 ml/¼ pint milk	⅔ cup milk
tablespoon grapefruit juice	1 tablespoon grapefruit juice
Garnish:	**Garnish:**
rapefruit segments	grapefruit segments
aprika pepper	paprika pepper

Vash, trim and cut the celery into 5 cm/2 inch
ieces. Cook in boiling salted water for
0 minutes. Drain and place in a shallow
erving dish. Keep hot.

Melt the margarine in a pan and stir in the
flour. Cook for 1 minute. Remove from the heat
and gradually blend in the milk. Heat, stirring,
until the sauce thickens. Stir in the grapefruit
juice and salt and pepper to taste. Cook for
1 minute then pour over the celery. Garnish
with grapefruit segments and paprika pepper.
Serve with meat or fish.
Cooking time: 20 minutes

Vegetable Layer

METRIC/IMPERIAL	AMERICAN
1 tablespoon oil	1 tablespoon oil
1 aubergine, sliced	1 eggplant, sliced
1 onion, sliced	1 onion, sliced
1 large leek, sliced	1 large leek, sliced
3 courgettes, sliced	3 zucchini, sliced
75 g/3 oz cheese, grated	¾ cup grated cheese
salt and pepper	salt and pepper
150 ml/¼ pint tomato juice	⅔ cup tomato juice

Heat the oil in a pan and sauté the aubergine
(eggplant) and onion for 5 minutes.

In a greased 1.2 litre/2 pint (5 cup) casserole
dish, layer the aubergine (eggplant) and onion
with the leek and courgettes (zucchini).
Sprinkle each layer with cheese and plenty of
salt and pepper. Pour over the tomato juice.

Cover tightly and cook in a preheated
moderate oven (180°C/350°F, Gas Mark 4) for
45 minutes to 1 hour until the vegetables are
tender. Serve hot or cold.
Cooking time: 50 minutes to 1 hour 5 minutes

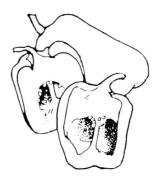

Desserts

Here is a selection of delicious desserts to make the perfect ending to a meal. The use of some convenience foods speeds up the preparation and avoids any waste. For ideas on imaginative ways to use fresh fruit and convenience foods, see the quick desserts at the end of this chapter.

Apricot and Raspberry Glories

METRIC/IMPERIAL	AMERICAN
1 × 425 g/15 oz can apricot halves	1 × 16 oz can apricot halves
1 packet raspberry jelly	1 package raspberry-flavored gelatin
150 ml/¼ pint hot water	⅔ cup hot water
300 ml/½ pint plain yogurt	1¼ cups plain yogurt
2 tablespoons clear honey	2 tablespoons honey
2 cherries to decorate	2 cherries to decorate

Drain the juice from the apricots and make up to 300 ml/½ pint (1¼ cups) with water. Reserve two apricot halves and slice the remainder.

Dissolve the jelly (gelatin) in the hot water, then stir in the fruit juice. Pour into a shallow container and chill until set. Turn the jelly out on to a wetted surface and, with a wet knife, chop it into small dice.

Mix together the yogurt and honey until they are well blended.

Layer the jelly, apricot slices and yogurt mixture in two large glasses. Decorate each with an apricot half and a cherry. Serve chilled.

Note: This recipe serves 2 people generously or will serve 4 if spooned into smaller glasses.

Blackcurrant Fool Crunch

METRIC/IMPERIAL	AMERICAN
225 g/8 oz fresh or frozen blackcurrants	2 cups fresh or frozen blackcurrants
1 tablespoon water	1 tablespoon water
1 tablespoon sugar	1 tablespoon sugar
1 × 170 g/6 oz can ready-made custard	1 × 6 oz can Bird's English Dessert Mix
25 g/1 oz butter	2 tablespoons butter
100 g/4 oz digestive biscuits, crushed	1½ cups graham cracker crumbs
whipped cream to decorate (optional)	whipped cream to decorate (optional)

Place the blackcurrants in a pan with the water and sugar. Heat gently until the fruit is tender. Cool, then rub the fruit through a sieve or purée in a blender or food processor.

Place the custard in a bowl and blend in the blackcurrant purée.

Melt the butter in a pan then stir in the biscuit (cracker) crumbs and mix well.

Place alternate layers of biscuit and blackcurrant mixture in glass serving dishes, finishing with the blackcurrants. Pipe whipped cream on top if wished. Serve chilled.
Cooking time: 15 minutes

Apricot and Raspberry Glories
(Photograph: John West Foods Limited)

Yogurt Banana Whip

METRIC/IMPERIAL	AMERICAN
2 small bananas	2 small bananas
40 g/1½ oz caster sugar	3 tablespoons sugar
2 teaspoons lemon juice	2 teaspoons lemon juice
25 g/1 oz almonds, finely chopped	¼ cup finely chopped almonds
2 teaspoons chopped stem ginger	2 teaspoons chopped preserved ginger
150 g/5 oz plain yogurt	⅔ cup plain yogurt
chocolate vermicelli to decorate	chocolate vermicelli to decorate

Mash the bananas and place in a pan with the sugar and lemon juice. Very slowly bring the mixture to the boil and continue to cook gently for 10 minutes.

Remove the pan from the heat and allow the mixture to cool. Stir in the nuts, ginger and yogurt. Blend well together then spoon into two individual serving dishes. Just before serving, decorate with the chocolate vermicelli.
Cooking time: 10 minutes

Pear and Chocolate Surprise

METRIC/IMPERIAL	AMERICAN
50 g/2 oz plain chocolate	2 squares (1 oz each) semi-sweet chocolate
1 × 175 g/6 oz can sterilized cream	1 × 6 oz can sterilized cream
4 slices chocolate Swiss roll	4 slices chocolate jelly roll
1 × 210 g/7½ oz can pear halves, drained	1 × 7½ oz can pear halves, drained
2 walnuts to decorate	2 walnuts to decorate

Break the chocolate into small pieces and place in a bowl over a pan of hot water. Stir gently until the chocolate has melted. Remove the bowl from the saucepan and allow the chocolate to cool a little. Stir in the cream and beat thoroughly.

Place the slices of Swiss (jelly) roll in two glass serving dishes. Place a pear half on top and pour the chocolate sauce over. Decorate each dessert with a walnut and serve.
Cooking time: 5 minutes

Hot Zabaglione

METRIC/IMPERIAL	AMERICAN
egg yolks	2 egg yolks
½ tablespoons caster sugar	1½ tablespoons caster sugar
tablespoons sweet sherry	6 tablespoons sweet sherry

lace the egg yolks, sugar and sherry in a
medium-sized bowl over a pan of gently
immering water. Whisk for about 8 to 10
minutes until thick and creamy. Pour into two
erving glasses and serve immediately.
ooking time: 8 to 10 minutes

Cold Zabaglione

METRIC/IMPERIAL	AMERICAN
0 g/2 oz granulated sugar	¼ cup sugar
tablespoons water	6 tablespoons water
egg yolks	2 egg yolks
tablespoon sweet sherry	1 tablespoon sweet sherry
tablespoons double cream, whipped	6 tablespoons heavy cream, whipped

lace the sugar and water in a pan and bring to
he boil. Boil until a thick syrup is formed. Place
he egg yolks in a bowl and gradually whisk in
he syrup and sherry. Continue whisking until
he mixture is thick and creamy. Fold in the
vhipped cream and spoon into serving dishes.
erve chilled.
ooking time: 5 minutes

Raspberry and Apple Fluff

METRIC/IMPERIAL	AMERICAN
2 egg whites	2 egg whites
25 g/1 oz caster sugar	2 tablespoons sugar
1 × 130 g/4½ oz can apple purée	1 × 4½ oz can applesauce
2 teaspoons lemon juice	2 teaspoons lemon juice
175 g/6 oz fresh or frozen raspberries	1 cup fresh or frozen raspberries
sponge fingers to serve	lady fingers to serve

Whisk the egg whites until stiff, then lightly fold
in the sugar. Place the apple in a bowl and stir
in the lemon juice. Gently fold in the egg whites
with a metal spoon.

Place the raspberries in the bottom of two
glass dishes, then top with the apple mixture.
Serve immediately with sponge (lady) fingers.

Crunchy Rhubarb Bake

METRIC/IMPERIAL	AMERICAN
350 g/12 oz rhubarb	¾ lb rhubarb
50 g/2 oz demerara sugar	⅓ cup brown sugar
1 orange	1 orange
2 large slices white bread (1 cm/½ inch thick)	2 large slices white bread (½ inch thick)
25 g/1 oz butter	2 tablespoons butter
½ teaspoon ground cinnamon	½ teaspoon ground cinnamon

Cut the rhubarb into 1 cm (½ inch) pieces and place in a 600 ml/1 pint (2½ cup) shallow ovenproof dish. Sprinkle with half the sugar.

Grate the rind from the orange and reserve. Squeeze the juice from the orange and pour it over the rhubarb. Remove the crusts from the slices of bread, then cut the bread into 1 cm (½ inch) cubes.

Melt the butter in a frying pan and add the orange rind and cinnamon. Add the bread cubes and toss in the butter. Arrange on top of the rhubarb and then sprinkle with the remaining sugar.

Cook in a preheated moderate oven (180°C/350°F, Gas Mark 4) for 45 minutes until the bread is golden brown. Serve hot with lightly whipped cream.

Cooking time: 45 minutes

Variation:

Use any fruit in season such as apples, gooseberries, apricots or plums.

Caribbean Coffee Creams

METRIC/IMPERIAL	AMERICAN
150 ml/¼ pint milk	⅔ cup milk
50 g/2 oz butter	¼ cup butter
25 g/1 oz cornflour	¼ cup cornstarch
1½ teaspoons instant coffee	1½ teaspoons instant coffee
25 g/1 oz soft brown sugar	1½ tablespoons soft brown sugar
3 sponge fingers	3 lady fingers
2 teaspoons rum essence	2 teaspoons rum extract
2 tablespoons water	2 tablespoons water
4 tablespoons double cream	4 tablespoons heavy cream
2 small chocolate flakes to decorate	2 small chocolate flakes to decorate

Place the milk, 25 g/1 oz (2 tablespoons) butter, cornflour (cornstarch) and coffee in a pan. Heat, whisking until the sauce thickens. Continue to cook, stirring continuously, for 1 minute. Cover and leave to cool.

Cream the remaining butter with the sugar, then slowly whisk into the cooled sauce. Fill a piping (pastry) bag, fitted with a fluted nozzle, with the mixture and place in the refrigerator.

Break up the sponge (lady) fingers. Mix together the rum essence (extract) and water and use to moisten them.

Whip the cream until thick. In two glass dishes, layer the sponge (lady) fingers and cream and coffee mixture ending with a piped whirl of coffee mixture on top. Chill in the refrigerator. Place a chocolate flake in each dessert and serve.

Cooking time: 10 minutes

Caribbean Coffee Creams
(Photograph: Cadbury Typhoo Food Advisory Service)

Mock Chocolate Mousse

METRIC/IMPERIAL
2 teaspoons custard
   powder
2 teaspoons sugar
150 ml/¼ pint milk
100 g/4 oz cooking
   chocolate
120 ml/4 fl oz single
   cream
grated chocolate to
   decorate

AMERICAN
2 teaspoons Bird's
   English Dessert Mix
2 teaspoons sugar
⅔ cup milk
4 squares (1 oz each)
   semi-sweet
   chocolate
½ cup light cream
grated chocolate to
   decorate

Blend the custard powder (Dessert Mix) and sugar with a little of the cold milk. Heat the remaining milk until almost boiling, then pour onto the custard mixture. Stir and return to the pan. Heat gently, stirring, until the sauce thickens, then continue to cook for 1 minute. Allow to cool.

Break up the chocolate and place in a bowl over a pan of gently simmering water. Stir until the chocolate has melted. Whisk the melted chocolate into the custard (Dessert Mix) with the cream and spoon into two serving dishes; chill. Decorate with grated chocolate and serve.
Cooking time: 15 minutes

Citrus Layer

METRIC/IMPERIAL
40 g/1½ oz butter
100 g/4 oz fresh brown
   breadcrumbs
20 g/¾ oz demerara
   sugar
grated rind of
   ½ orange
½ × 312 g/11 oz can
   mandarin orange
   segments, drained
150 ml/¼ pint double
   cream
1 teaspoon grated
   lemon rind
2 teaspoons lemon
   juice

AMERICAN
3 tablespoons butter
2 cups soft brown
   bread crumbs
1 tablespoon brown
   sugar
grated rind of
   ½ orange
½ × 11 oz can
   mandarin orange
   segments, drained
⅔ cup heavy cream
1 teaspoon grated
   lemon rind
2 teaspoons lemon
   juice

Melt the butter in a pan and fry the breadcrumbs until crisp. Allow to cool, then stir in the sugar and orange rind.

Reserve a few mandarins for decoration and rub the remainder through a sieve or purée in a blender or food processor. Whip the cream until thick and fold into the mandarin purée with the lemon rind and juice.

Place alternate layers of breadcrumbs and cream mixture in two tall glasses. Decorate with the reserved mandarins and serve chilled.
Cooking time: 5 minutes

Strawberry Jelly Cream

METRIC/IMPERIAL	AMERICAN
¾ packet strawberry jelly	¾ package strawberry-flavored gelatin
1 × 383 g/13½ oz can strawberries	1 × 13½ oz can strawberries
juice of ½ lemon	juice of ½ lemon
2 tablespoons soured cream	2 tablespoons sour cream

Break up the jelly and place in a pan. Strain in the juice from the strawberries. Heat gently to dissolve the jelly. Allow to cool a little then stir in the lemon juice and strawberries, reserving a few for decoration. Add the sour cream and blend well. Leave until just beginning to set, then stir to evenly distribute the strawberries. Spoon into two serving glasses. Leave to set, then decorate with the remaining strawberries.
Cooking time: 10 minutes

Jamaican Meringue

METRIC/IMPERIAL	AMERICAN
15 g/½ oz brown sugar	1 tablespoon brown sugar
25 g/1 oz butter	2 tablespoons butter
juice of 1 lemon	juice of 1 lemon
1 tablespoon rum	1 tablespoon rum
2 egg whites	2 egg whites
25 g/1 oz caster sugar	2 tablespoons sugar
25 g/1 oz desiccated coconut	⅓ cup shredded coconut
2 bananas	2 bananas

Place the brown sugar and butter in a pan and heat gently until melted, then stir in the lemon juice and rum.

Whisk the egg whites until stiff, then fold in the sugar and coconut.

Peel the bananas and slice lengthwise, then arrange in a shallow buttered ovenproof dish. Pour over the rum sauce and top with the meringue. Cook in a preheated moderate oven (180°C/350°F, Gas Mark 4) for 10 to 15 minutes. Serve immediately.
Cooking time: 15 to 20 minutes

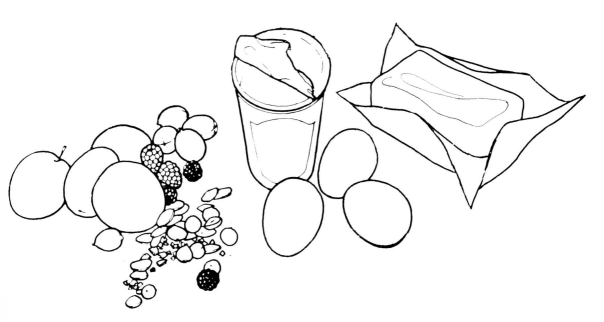

Orange Yogurt Sorbet (Sherbet)

METRIC/IMPERIAL	AMERICAN
2 small oranges	2 small oranges
300 ml/½ pint plain yogurt	1¼ cups plain yogurt
120 ml/4 fl oz unsweetened orange juice	½ cup unsweetened orange juice
1 tablespoon powdered gelatine	1 tablespoon unflavored gelatin
4 tablespoons water	4 tablespoons water
2 egg whites	2 egg whites

If there is no freezer available, turn the refrigerator to the coldest setting.

Grate the zest from the oranges and mix with the yogurt and orange juice.

Sprinkle the gelatine over the water in a bowl. Place over a pan of gently simmering water and stir until dissolved. Cool and add to the yogurt mixture. Leave on one side.

Whisk the egg whites until stiff. When the yogurt mixture is beginning to set, fold in the egg whites. Pour into a shallow tray and freeze.

To serve, remove the remaining peel and pith from the oranges and slice them. Divide the sorbet (sherbet) between two sundae dishes and top with the orange slices.

Raspberry Creams

METRIC/IMPERIAL	AMERICAN
175 g/6 oz raspberries	1 cup raspberries
1 tablespoon kirsch (optional)	1 tablespoon kirsch (optional)
2 teaspoons custard powder	2 teaspoons Bird's English Dessert Mix
2 teaspoons sugar	2 teaspoons sugar
150 ml/¼ pint milk	⅔ cup milk
6 tablespoons double cream	6 tablespoons heavy cream

Reserve a few raspberries for decoration. Sprinkle the kirsch, if using, over the remaining raspberries and leave to stand for 2 hours. Rub the raspberries through a sieve or purée in a blender or food processor.

Blend the custard powder (Dessert Mix) and sugar with a little of the cold milk. Heat the remaining milk until almost boiling, then pour on to the custard mixture. Stir and return to the pan. Heat gently, stirring, until the sauce thickens, then continue to cook for 1 minute. Allow to cool.

Whip the cream until thick. Reserve a little for decoration and fold the remainder into the cold custard. Stir in the raspberry purée and blend well. Spoon into two dishes, decorate with the remaining cream and raspberries and serve chilled.

Cooking time: 10 minutes

*Raspberry Creams
(Photograph: Bird's Desserts)*

Blackberry Soufflé Omelette

METRIC/IMPERIAL	AMERICAN
2 eggs, separated	2 eggs, separated
1 teaspoon sugar	1 teaspoon sugar
15 g/½ oz butter	1 tablespoon butter
Filling:	**Filling:**
100 g/4 oz blackberries	¾ cup blackberries
1 tablespoon sugar	1 tablespoon sugar
2 tablespoons plain yogurt	2 tablespoons plain yogurt

To make the filling, place the blackberries and sugar in a pan and heat until the fruit is tender.

To make the omelette, mix the egg yolks with the sugar. Whisk the egg whites until stiff and fold into the yolks.

Melt the butter in a small frying pan and pour in the egg mixture. Cook for 3 to 4 minutes until firm underneath. Cook under a preheated moderate grill (broiler) until golden brown. Turn the omelette onto a serving plate and spoon the blackberries over one side. Fold over and cut into two. Serve each portion topped with a spoonful of yogurt.

Cooking time: 20 minutes

Crunchy Fruit Compote

METRIC/IMPERIAL	AMERICAN
225 g/8 oz mixed dried fruits	½ lb mixed dried fruits
150 ml/¼ pint water	⅔ cup water
1 tablespoon clear honey	1 tablespoon honey
juice of ½ lemon	juice of ½ lemon
40 g/1½ oz butter	3 tablespoons butter
25 g/1 oz demerara sugar	1½ tablespoons brown sugar
50 g/2 oz muesli cereal	½ cup granola

Place the dried fruits in a bowl, cover with cold water and leave to soak overnight. Drain well, then place in a pan with 150 ml/¼ pint (⅔ cup) fresh water, the honey and lemon juice. Bring to the boil, cover and cook gently for about 20 minutes until the fruit is tender. Turn into a 600 ml/1 pint (2½ cup) ovenproof dish.

Melt the butter in a pan and add the sugar and muesli (granola). Mix well then sprinkle over the fruits. Place under a preheated moderate grill (broiler) until golden brown. Serve warm with cream or yogurt.

Cooking time: 25 minutes

Quick Dessert Ideas

1. Melt 100 g/4 oz plain (semi-sweet) chocolate in a fondue pan. Dip pieces of chilled fresh fruit into it.

2. Soak 4 to 6 gingernut biscuits (cookies) in sherry, then place in a dish. Top with cubes of melon and whipped cream.

3. Scoop melon balls from quarter of a watermelon. Cut the fruit from half a pineapple and mix with the melon. Pour over 2 tablespoons of liqueur and pile into the empty pineapple shell.

4. Cut a small honeydew or galia melon in half and remove the seeds. Fill the hollows with fresh raspberries. Pour over a little sherry and sprinkle with sugar.

5. Place 100 g/4 oz (1 cup) seedless grapes in a small heatproof dish. Cover with 150ml/¼ pint (⅔ cup) sour cream. Chill for 2 hours. Sprinkle with 1 tablespoon soft brown sugar and place under a preheated grill (broiler) for 5 minutes until the sugar is bubbling.

6. Blend 150 ml/¼ pint (⅔ cup) whipped cream with the same amount of fruit yogurt. Place in two dishes and serve chilled and decorated with nuts.

7. Chill a small can of evaporated milk, then whisk until it thickens. Add the grated rind and juice of ½ lemon, 1 tablespoon sugar and 2 tablespoons plain yogurt. Mix well and divide between two glass dishes.

8. Mix together 4 tablespoons whipped cream and 4 tablespoons fruit yogurt. Whisk an egg white until stiff and fold into the mixture. Spoon into dishes and serve immediately.

9. Drain the juice from a small can of fruit salad. Place the fruit in a heatproof dish. Arrange 8 marshmallows on top and place under a preheated grill (broiler) until they begin to melt. Serve with plain yogurt or sour cream.

10. Arrange pieces of fresh fruit and marshmallows onto two kebab sticks. Serve with chocolate sauce, fruit purée or fruit yogurt.

11. Whisk 1 egg white and fold into 150 ml/¼ pint (⅔ cup) fruit purée. Spoon into two dishes and serve immediately.

12. Purée the fruit from half a watermelon with 300 ml/½ pint (1¼ cups) fresh orange juice in a blender or food processor. Place crushed ice in two tall glasses and pour over the juice. Top with a scoop of ice cream.

Entertaining

Try one of the following menus for a really delicious dinner for two.

Tomato Cups
Breton Rack
Canterbury Apples

Tomato Cups

METRIC/IMPERIAL	AMERICAN
2 large tomatoes	2 large tomatoes
25 g/1 oz butter	2 tablespoons butter
1 small onion, grated	1 small onion, minced
75 g/3 oz lambs' liver, thinly sliced	3 oz lamb liver, thinly sliced
1 teaspoon dried sage	1 teaspoon dried sage
salt and pepper	salt and pepper
watercress to garnish	watercress for garnish

Cut a slice from the top of each tomato and scoop out the flesh from inside and reserve, discard the core and seeds.

Melt the butter in a pan and sauté the onion for 5 minutes. Add the tomato pulp and the liver. Continue to cook for 5 minutes, then add the sage and salt and pepper to taste. Rub the tomato mixture through a sieve or purée in a blender or food processor. Use the mixture to fill the tomato shells. Chill in the refrigerator. Garnish with watercress and serve with toast.
Cooking time: 12 to 15 minutes

Breton Rack

METRIC/IMPERIAL	AMERICAN
1 best end of lamb, chined and trimmed	1 lamb rib roast, chined and trimmed
1 garlic clove, crushed	1 garlic clove, minced
2 tablespoons honey, melted	2 tablespoons honey, melted

Menu for two – Tomato Cups; Breton Rack; Canterbury Apples
(Photograph: New Zealand Lamb Information Bureau)

Crisp topping:

2 tablespoons fresh breadcrumbs	2 tablespoons soft bread crumbs
2 teaspoons chopped parsley	2 teaspoons chopped parsley
1 teaspoon chopped sage	1 teaspoon chopped sage
1 teaspoon crushed rosemary	1 teaspoon crushed rosemary
salt and pepper	salt and pepper
watercress to garnish	watercress for garnish

Cover bone tips of lamb with foil. Rub garlic into back of lamb and spread over honey.

Mix together the breadcrumbs, herbs, salt and pepper, then sprinkle them over the honey.

Cook in a preheated moderate oven (180°C/350°F, Gas Mark 4) for 1¼ to 1½ hours. Transfer to a warmed serving dish, garnish with watercress and serve with roast potatoes and a selection of vegetables in season.
Cooking time: 1¼ to 1½ hours

Canterbury Apples

METRIC/IMPERIAL	AMERICAN
2 large cooking apples	2 large tart apples
50 g/2 oz curd cheese	¼ cup small curd cottage cheese
25 g/1 oz sultanas	3 tablespoons raisins
25 g/1 oz brown sugar	2 tablespoons brown sugar
½ teaspoon ground cinnamon	½ teaspoon ground cinnamon

Remove the cores from apples and make a cut around the middle of each apple. Place in a greased, shallow ovenproof dish.

Blend together the curd cheese, sultanas (raisins), half the sugar and the cinnamon. Use the mixture to fill the centres of the apples. Sprinkle with the remaining sugar.

Cook in a preheated moderate oven (180°C/350°F, Gas Mark 4) for 1 hour. Serve hot.
Cooking time: 1 hour

Iced Avocado Soup with Chilli
Chicken Paprika
Toffee Meringue Glacé

Iced Avocado Soup with Chilli

METRIC/IMPERIAL	AMERICAN
1 avocado, peeled and stoned	1 avocado, peeled and seeded
2 tablespoons lemon juice	2 tablespoons lemon juice
½ chicken stock cube	1 chicken bouillon cube
4 tablespoons boiling water	4 tablespoons boiling water
150 ml/¼ pint plain yogurt	⅔ cup plain yogurt
3 drops Tabasco sauce	3 drops hot pepper sauce
salt and pepper	salt and pepper
Garnish:	**Garnish:**
1 iceberg lettuce, shredded	1 iceberg lettuce, shredded
yogurt	yogurt
chilli seasoning	chili seasoning

Purée the avocado and lemon juice in a blender or food processor.

Dissolve the stock (bouillon) cube in the water and leave to cool. Add to the avocado purée with most of the yogurt and the Tabasco (hot pepper) sauce. Mix well and add salt and pepper to taste.

Pour into serving bowls and chill. Serve topped with shredded lettuce, a spoonful of yogurt and a little chilli seasoning.

Chicken Paprika

METRIC/IMPERIAL	AMERICAN
25 g/1 oz butter	2 tablespoons butter
2 large chicken drumsticks	2 large chicken drumsticks
1 small onion, chopped	1 small onion, chopped
2 teaspoons paprika pepper	2 teaspoons paprika pepper
2 tomatoes, skinned and quartered	2 tomatoes, peeled and quartered
1 celery stick, chopped	1 stalk celery, chopped
25 g/1 oz mushrooms, sliced	¼ cup sliced mushrooms
½ green pepper, cored, seeded and chopped	½ green pepper, seeded and chopped
150 ml/¼ pint chicken stock	⅔ cup chicken stock
salt and pepper	salt and pepper
3 tablespoons soured cream	3 tablespoons sour cream
2 teaspoons plain flour	2 teaspoons all-purpose flour
parsley sprigs to garnish	parsley sprigs for garnish

Melt the butter in a pan and fry the chicken until browned on all sides. Remove from the pan with a slotted spoon and set aside. Sauté the onion for 3 minutes, then add the paprika and cook for 1 minute.

Add the tomatoes, celery, mushrooms, green pepper, stock, and salt and pepper to taste. Bring to the boil, cover and simmer for 45 minutes. Remove the chicken from the sauce and place on a warmed serving dish.

Blend the cream and flour together and add to the sauce. Heat, stirring, until the sauce thickens. Continue to cook for 1 minute without boiling, then pour over the chicken. Garnish with parsley and serve with boiled rice and a mixed salad.
Cooking time: 55 minutes

Toffee Meringue Glacé

METRIC/IMPERIAL	AMERICAN
2 meringue nests	2 meringue nests
2 scoops vanilla ice cream	2 scoops vanilla ice cream
Sauce:	**Sauce:**
2 tablespoons brown sugar	2 tablespoons brown sugar
2 teaspoons golden syrup	2 teaspoons light corn syrup
1 tablespoon milk	1 tablespoon milk
15 g/½ oz butter	1 tablespoon butter
½ teaspoon vanilla essence	½ teaspoon vanilla

To make the sauce, place all the ingredients in a pan. Heat gently, stirring, to dissolve the sugar, then bring to the boil. Continue to boil for 3 to 4 minutes, stirring continuously.

Place the meringues on two serving dishes. Just before serving, place the ice cream in the centre and spoon a little of the sauce over the top. Serve the remaining sauce separately.
Cooking time: 5 minutes

Champignons en Cocotte
Sweet and Sour Pork with
Chinese Prawns (Shrimp)
Melon Sherry Cups

Champignons en Cocotte

METRIC/IMPERIAL	AMERICAN
100 g/4 oz button mushrooms	1 cup button mushrooms
15 g/½ oz butter	1 tablespoon butter
salt and freshly ground black pepper	salt and freshly ground black pepper
150 ml/¼ pint double cream	⅔ cup heavy cream
25 g/1 oz Parmesan cheese, grated	¼ cup grated Parmesan cheese
parsley sprigs to garnish	parsley sprigs for garnish

Divide the mushrooms between two buttered ramekin dishes, then dot with butter. Sprinkle with salt and pepper, then pour over cream.

Top with the Parmesan cheese and place in a preheated moderately hot oven (190°C/375°F, Gas Mark 5) for 10 to 15 minutes. Garnish with parsley sprigs and serve with Melba toast.
Cooking time: 10 to 15 minutes

Sweet and Sour Pork with Chinese Prawns (Shrimp)

METRIC/IMPERIAL	AMERICAN
25 g/1 oz margarine	2 tablespoons margarine
225 g/8 oz pork fillet, diced	½ lb pork tenderloin, diced
300 ml/½ pint chicken stock	1¼ cups chicken stock
1 bouquet garni	1 bouquet garni
2 teaspoons cornflour	2 teaspoons cornstarch
1 tablespoon vinegar	1 tablespoon vinegar
2 teaspoons soy sauce	2 teaspoons soy sauce
1 teaspoon tomato purée	1 teaspoon tomato paste
2 teaspoons sugar	2 teaspoons sugar
1 carrot, chopped	1 carrot, chopped
½ green pepper, cored, seeded and sliced	½ green pepper, seeded and sliced
salt and pepper	salt and pepper
1 × 260 g/9½ oz can beansprouts	1 × 9½ oz can beansprouts

Chinese Prawns:

2 teaspoons cornflour	
150 ml/¼ pint stock	
2 teaspoons soy sauce	
75 g/3 oz cauliflower, cut into florets	
2 tablespoons chopped cucumber	
1 red pepper, cored, seeded and sliced	
75 g/3 oz peeled prawns	
salt and pepper	

Chinese Shrimp:

2 teaspoons cornstarch	
⅔ cup stock	
2 teaspoons soy sauce	
3 oz cauliflower, cut into florets	
2 tablespoons chopped cucumber	
1 red pepper, seeded and sliced	
½ cup shelled shrimp	
salt and pepper	

Melt the margarine in a pan and fry the pork until evenly browned all over. Add the stock and bouquet garni. Bring to the boil, cover and simmer for 30 minutes.

Blend the cornflour (cornstarch) with the vinegar, soy sauce, tomato purée (paste) and sugar. Add to the pan with the carrot and green pepper. Add salt and pepper to taste, then heat until the sauce thickens. Continue to cook the pork mixture for 15 to 20 minutes.

In a separate pan, heat the beansprouts and drain. Place in a serving dish and keep hot.

To make the Chinese prawns (shrimp): blend the cornflour (cornstarch) with the cooled stock and add the soy sauce. Heat, stirring, until the sauce thickens.

Add the cauliflower, cucumber and red pepper, and then continue to simmer for 10 minutes. Stir in the prawns (shrimp) and salt and pepper to taste. Heat through thoroughly and transfer to a warmed serving dish.

Spoon the pork over the beansprouts and serve the two dishes with boiled rice.
Cooking time: 1 hour 20 minutes

Melon Sherry Cups

METRIC/IMPERIAL	AMERICAN
1 medium Ogen melon	1 medium Ogen melon
2 teaspoons finely grated orange rind	2 teaspoons finely grated orange rind
2 teaspoons sherry	2 teaspoons sherry
4 maraschino cherries	4 maraschino cherries

Cut the melon in half and remove the seeds. Scoop out the flesh with a melon baller or teaspoon and place in a bowl. Add the orange rind and sherry and mix well.

Spoon the melon mixture back into the melon halves and decorate with the cherries. Chill before serving. Serve with cream.

Asparagus Soup

METRIC/IMPERIAL	AMERICAN
15 g/½ oz butter	1 tablespoon butter
15 g/½ oz plain flour	2 tablespoons all-purpose flour
300 ml/½ pint milk	1¼ cups milk
150 ml/¼ pint stock	⅔ cup stock
1 × 340 g/12 oz can asparagus, drained	1 × 12 oz can asparagus, drained
salt and pepper	salt and pepper

Melt the butter in a pan, stir in the flour and cook for 1 minute. Remove from the heat and gradually blend in the milk and stock. Heat, stirring, until the soup thickens a little. Add the asparagus, reserving two tips for garnish. Simmer for 5 minutes. Rub the mixture through a sieve, or purée in a blender or food processor. Add salt and pepper to taste.

Reheat the soup and pour into two warmed bowls. Garnish with the reserved asparagus. Cooking time: 20 minutes

Celebration Seafood Pie

METRIC/IMPERIAL	AMERICAN
Pastry:	**Dough:**
100 g/4 oz plain flour	1 cup all-purpose flour
pinch of salt	pinch of salt
25 g/1 oz margarine	2 tablespoons margarine
25 g/1 oz lard	2 tablespoons shortening
1 tablespoon water	1 tablespoon water
beaten egg to glaze	beaten egg for glaze
Filling:	**Filling:**
150 ml/¼ pint milk	⅔ cup milk
175 g/6 oz cod, cubed	6 oz cod, cubed
15 g/½ oz butter	1 tablespoon butter
15 g/½ oz plain flour	2 tablespoons all-purpose flour
150 ml/¼ pint dry white wine	⅔ cup dry white wine
75 g/3 oz peeled prawns	½ cup shelled shrimp
1 × 99 g/3½ oz can pink salmon, drained and flaked	1 × 3½ oz can pink salmon, drained and flaked
1 tablespoon chopped parsley	1 tablespoon chopped parsley
salt and pepper	salt and pepper

Sift the flour and salt into a bowl and rub (cut) in the margarine and lard (shortening) until the mixture resembles fine breadcrumbs. Add the water and mix to a firm dough. Knead lightly on a floured surface until the dough is smooth. Chill in the refrigerator.

To make the filling: place the milk and fish in a pan and poach for 10 minutes. Strain and reserve the liquor.

Melt the butter in a pan, stir in the flour and cook for 1 minute. Remove from the heat and gradually blend in the fish liquor and wine. Heat, stirring, until the sauce thickens. Continue to cook for 1 minute, then stir in the cod, prawns (shrimp), salmon and parsley. Add salt and pepper to taste. Place in a 600 ml/1 pint (2½ cup) pie dish (pan) and leave to cool.

Roll out the pastry to a circle larger than the dish. Cut a strip 1 cm/½ inch wide from the edge and place around the moistened rim of the pie dish. Moisten the strip and place the pastry over the top to make a lid. Trim, seal and flute the edges. Roll out any trimmings and cut into fish shapes. Moisten these and place on top of the pie. Brush with beaten egg.

Cook in a preheated moderately hot oven (200°C/400°F, Gas Mark 6) for 20 minutes until the top is cooked and golden. Serve hot with French fries, peas and baked tomatoes. Cooking time: 40 minutes

Lemon Delight

METRIC/IMPERIAL	AMERICAN
2 egg whites	2 egg whites
25 g/1 oz ratafias, crushed	¼ cup crushed ratafias
6 tablespoons double cream	6 tablespoons heavy cream
grated rind and juice of 1 small lemon	grated rind and juice of 1 small lemon
3 tablespoons Marsala	3 tablespoons Marsala
2 tablespoons caster sugar	2 tablespoons sugar
chocolate curls to decorate	chocolate curls to decorate

Brush the inside of two glass dishes with some of the egg white and coat with the ratafias.

Whip the cream until thick, then stir in the lemon rind and juice, Marsala and sugar. Whisk the remaining egg whites until stiff and fold into the lemon cream. Spoon into the dishes and chill well. Decorate with chocolate curls before serving.

Index

The publishers wish to acknowledge the following photographers – Paul Williams: cover. Roger Phillips: page 2. Graham T. Langridge: pages 6 and 18. Paul Williams: pages 23, 27, 34 and 39.
Illustrations by Mary Tomlin.

PDO 82-0164